CONSTITUTIONAL ARRANGEMENTS OF THE REPUBLIC OF GHANA AND FEDERAL REPUBLIC OF NIGERIA, 1844 -1992

2nd and Revised Edition With index

ALISON KWAME DEIMA-NYAHO

PARTRIDGE

To order additional copies of this book, contact
Toll Free +65 3165 7531 (Singapore)
Toll Free +60 3 3099 4412 (Malaysia)
orders.singapore@partridgepublishing.com

www.partridgepublishing.com/singapore

CONTENTS

PREFACE TO THE SECOND REVISED EDITION

The constitutional journeys of Ghana and Nigeria have had checkered histories. However, in a way, these countries may congratulate themselves for having traveled the journey so far, even though the tides have not been smooth sailing all along, as is to be expected.

The Constitution of the Republic of Ghana (1992), in particular, would seek to play a landmark role in the sense that it purported to provide for all situations that human experience could call to mind. It also would seek to provide for possible situations that can be anticipated. This is quite understandable because life in this age is so complex that reliance on only scientific knowledge and method or what can be proved alone is not enough. The late twentieth-century world was overwhelmed with a shocking fact that human beings were detonating themselves in the Middle East in what has come to be commonly known as suicide bombing. In the light of this reality, it should have possibly occurred to the world that there could also be suicide skyjacking for the purpose for which it was employed on September 11, 2001, in the United States of America and preemptive or preventive measures taken within the framework of the freedoms enjoyed by Americans. Human knowledge and experience had not encompassed a situation where people could hijack airplanes, use them as missiles, and smash them deliberately into buildings with the intention of causing maximum damage before it took place. There are certain things and situations that cannot be explained by reason. Constitutional provisions are expected as guides for governance in human societies to bring about harmonious development and the well-being of all.

While the scope and purport of the substantial work remain the same and unchanged, new emphases are placed on articles discussing patriotism, nationalism, statesmanship, and education for eradication of illiteracy, ignorance, and poverty; the Nigerian Civil War and its aftermath; the efforts and their failures to avoid the civil war itself; and the chance for improving the mindset and thought processes of heterogeneous ethnic divergences to be able to succeed in making a stable and peaceable nation-state in West Africa in particular in spite of inimical influences of former European colonial powers.

Nigeria is a federation, while Ghana is a unitary republic. Both, however, derive their common experiences in governance from Britain as well as empirical occurrences. It is in this context that all can view these constitutional provisions as well as their backgrounds.

Readers are therefore implored to look at the issues discussed in this work without prejudices. The paramount aim is still to set the records straight and not to denigrate and also to create awareness so that no tyrannical dictator should get an opportunity to rise up again anywhere any day. For an oppressor's rule, if it would appear, can best be prevented and not resisted conveniently. The general concern should therefore be to identify those facts, which in the past tended to create room for dictatorship of any kind—civilian, military, or an admixture of both—and to avoid them. It has to be admitted that there is something nasty about the human species: the tendency to be absolutely domineering to the exclusion and the consideration of other people's views or interests—a situation that should not be allowed to manifest in persons trusted with top leadership positions in governance. That is what successive constitutional arrangements in Ghana and Nigeria, especially in the former, have sought to achieve.

If this book succeeds in its selected objective, I am most grateful to all those who have complimented my effort with critical observations as well as their perspectives. They are therefore entitled to share in the glory that only success can bring. In this respect, I feel a strong obligation to mention with profound gratitude Mr. G. K. Letsu, for his critical perspectives and encouragement; my two university-graduate sons, Setorwu and Mawuduji, now fully matured, who contributed intellectually in critical and dispassionate examination, objectively evaluating the ideas and principles canvassed in this work; Mr. Umar Graham-Mensa, for his most infectious zeal to convert my manuscript into type; and Mr. Philipo Nyaho-Datti, for his special interest. The secretarial duties in connection with this second revised edition were performed by Hajia Maimuna of MI Horizon Ghana Limited, Zongo Junction, Madina, Accra. I am, however, entirely and personally responsible for any flaws and shortcomings that may be found in this work by any reader.

CHAPTER ONE

HISTORICAL LANDMARKS

There has never been any doubt that Africans, in their heterogeneity, lived in forms of organized societies in their own ways prior to the contact made with European visitors of different nationalities to the continent.

The context of the people of Ghana and Nigeria in West Africa cannot be different. However, the various tribal groups had problems about them that cannot be denied. While they were not at peace with their tribal neighbors, they were also not at peace with themselves within their various tribal habitations. In addition, some of the tribal habitations were not in units contiguous enough to make nation-states by definition. Thus, except the Akans of Ghana (Fanti and Twi tribes together), the Ewe people of Ghana and Togo, the Hausa-Fulani people, and the Ibos and Yoruba people, these tribes as individual tribal units cannot make separate nation-states. The tribal units also suffered from certain barbaric practices, which quite often promoted civil unrest and violent clashes. In this state, the European visitors to the continent made contact with them in the nineteenth century the first time to institutionalize governance.

The first documented evidence in connection with such European contact with Africans west of the continent is the Bond of 1844 concluded at

Cape Coast[1] in the then Gold Coast. When the content of this document, which W. E. Ward only refers to as the "Bond of 1844" in his book *A Short History of the Gold Coast*, is examined, it becomes safe then to deduce that the European visitors must have condoned or contributed or even aided in various ways those tribal unrests in the west coast of Africa prior to the sixth of March 1844, for the bond states as follows:

> Bond, 6th March 1844:
> 1. Whereas power and jurisdiction have been exercised for and on behalf of Her Majesty the Queen of Great Britain and Ireland within diverse countries and places adjacent to her Majesty's Forts and Settlements on the Gold Coast, we the Chiefs of countries and places so referred to, adjacent to the said Forts and Settlements, do hereby acknowledge that power and jurisdiction and declare that the first objects of governance are the protection of individuals and of property.
> 2. Human sacrifices and barbarous customs such as panyaring,[2] are abominations and contrary to law.
> 3. Murders, robberies and other crimes and offences will be tried and enquired of before the Queen's judicial officers and the chiefs of the districts, moulding the customs of the country to the general principles of the British law.
>
> Done at Cape Coast Castle before His Excellency the Lieutenant Governor on this 6th day of March, in the year of our Lord 1844.

This bond was made between one H. W. Hill, who was the lieutenant governor, and some eight coastal chiefs who made their right thumbprints to authenticate it before three witnesses, namely:

---

1 John Mensah Sarbah, *Fanti Customary Laws*, pp. 231 et seq; T. O. S. Elias, "Law and Social Change in Nigeria and Nigerian Legal System."

2 Panyaring was a system whereby a native of a tribe or clan in debt was seized by the creditor clan until the debt was paid or settled or the victim sold in settlement of the debt.

1. George MacLean, JP and assessor
2. F. Pogsun, First WI Regiment Commanding HM Troops
3. S. Bannerman, adjutant of the militia and police

It would appear that the Bond of 1844 sought to do two things. The first purpose would appear to be to legitimize or legalize the status of the British settlements in the Gold Coast Colony and, in the process, to rectify their unsatisfactory state of affairs as the Europeans or the Britons found it as the result of their contact with the Africans living there. But this second purpose was an inevitable or necessary concomitant of the first purpose, which was to create an atmosphere that would be conducive to their activities and would produce as much as practicable conditions similar to what they were used to in Britain.

Further to this bond in the Gold Coast Colony (now Ghana), the British government appointed a British consul in Nigeria in 1849. The consul was to oversee the interests of British merchants on the coasts of Nigeria. From this point on, a marked difference is to be noted in the approaches to the way the Britons handled their affairs in the two countries.

Ghana

In 1850, a legislative council was set up to advise the colonial governor in enacting laws for the Gold Coast Colony and in drawing up the colony's budget. But the primary functions of the Legislative Council were purely advisory. The governor had all the legislative and executive powers vested in him, and he was not bound to follow the advice of the council. The governor himself nominated the members of the Legislative Council. This position lasted until 1916 when the Legislative Council was reconstituted. There were now six Africans among the nine members nominated by the governor, and only three of them were officials. This was opposed to the 1850 arrangement of eleven nominated officials, which included the governor himself.

The Guggisberg Constitutional Arrangement

In 1925, under Governor Sir Gordon Guggisberg (2), the unofficial membership of the Legislative Council was increased to fourteen. The Provincial Council of Chiefs elected six out of this number. Three were elected as municipal members representing Accra, Cape Coast, and Sekondi, being elected by ratepayers, while five were nominated European officials. The total number of officials was increased to fifteen, inclusive of the governor. However, while the governor had full control over the Legislative Council, the elective principle was introduced for the first time in the Gold Coast under Governor Guggisberg.

In 1946, under Governor Sir Alan Burns, the Guggisberg Arrangement was replaced. The new arrangement that took its place introduced for the first time in the Legislative Council a majority of Africans, even though not all that majority were elected. Under the Burns Arrangement, there were eighteen African members of the council comprising thirteen elected by the Council of Chiefs while urban electorates (i.e., ratepayers or property owners) elected five. Although the governor retained some vital powers—for example, the powers of certification (assent) and veto—the secretary of state and the executive were responsible to him and not to the Legislative Council. It can be said that the Burns Constitution was at the time the most advanced constitutional arrangement in tropical Africa.

Following some disturbances that took place two years after the introduction of the Burns Constitutional Arrangement (i.e., in 1948), the Watson Commission and the Coussey Committee advised that there should be a constitution that should place the responsibility for framing and executing policy on the Africans, thereby reducing British control. This notwithstanding, the governor still retained his powers of certification and veto. Thus by 1951, the new Constitution gave the Gold Coast a limited responsible government by enabling elected ministers to head departments. And by 1954, the Constitution provided for a legislative assembly of a speaker and 104 members all elected on party lines based on universal adult suffrage, without any special members. No member of the Legislative Assembly was nominated in 1951 and 1954. So the Gold Coast had an elected National Assembly, which could be called a Parliament (a House of Commons). There were eight ministries headed by Africans, which did not include defense and external affairs.

The Independence Constitution of Ghana made the governor a nominal head of state representing the Queen of Britain who gave his assent to bills to become law. The whole arrangement was patterned on the principles and conventions that were obtained in Britain. Nevertheless, three years later, the nationalist government decided to change that constitutional arrangement into a Republican type of government, and the Republican Constitution of 1960 established the position of executive presidency, whereby Kwame Nkrumah became the entrenched executive president.

It is significant to note that it was provided in the 1960 Republican Constitution of Ghana that

1. the Powers of government spring from the will of the people and should be exercised in accordance therewith;
2. freedom and justice should be honoured and maintained;
3. no person shall suffer discrimination on grounds of sex, race, tribe, religion or political belief;
4. chieftaincy in Ghana should be guaranteed and preserved . . .

However, it was on the basis of the following provision, "Subject to such restrictions as may be necessary for preserving public order, morality or health, no person shall be deprived of freedom of religion or speech, of the right to move and assembly without hindrance or of the right of access to Courts of Law," that the fortuitous leader of the country was enabled to trample on the provisions guaranteeing the above freedoms to the people. As a result, the Preventive Detention Act (PDA) was enacted just a year after Ghana attained independence, with which the government virtually terrorized the citizenry; hence, the determination of that government by a coup d'état in 1966 was greeted by the majority of the people with celebration and jubilation. This was so because intellectual honesty cannot run away from the fact that the overambition of Nkrumah, subsequent to the enactment of the PDA, conveniently ignored or forgot that on the arrest of Nkrumah and keeping him in prison and also the simultaneous release of Gbedemah from prison in 1949, the leadership of the CPP became the responsibility of K. A. Gbedemah in the interim. Gbedemah spearheaded the independence struggle throughout the Gold Coast as the interim leader of the CPP until Nkrumah was released from prison in 1951. Gbedemah thus carried the original UGCC message, which now became adopted by the CPP: "Our aim and purpose were to put together colony and Ashanti, Togoland and the Northern Territories and then to manage our own affairs and shed the colonial yoke." The colonial administration eventually yielded under pressure and ordered a general election in 1951. The interim CPP leadership under Gbedemah insisted that although in prison custody, Nkrumah should be allowed to stand as a candidate in that election, being convinced that he would win and then be released from prison.

Some well-meaning individuals, however, foresaw very early the tyrannically totalitarian proclivity of Kwame Nkrumah, but a number of factors contributed to the tyrannical dictatorship experienced by Ghanaians between 1958 and 1966. It is necessary to identify and examine those factors for their prevention in constitutional arrangements and also look at contemporary actions that took place in Nigeria at the time. What is noteworthy now though is that there had been concerted and conscious efforts by the people of West Africa toward shedding the colonial yoke or gaining political freedom from any perceived oppression or suppression of any kind many years prior to the two world wars of 1914 and 1939–1945.

CHAPTER TWO

REORIENTING THE DEMOCRATIC PATH

In light of the foregoing, therefore, there is the need to face the fact that the absence of intellectual honesty is the cause of the major political problems facing Africa and Ghana. All leadership problems in Africa often arise because people tend to distort facts and colour—issues to suit their prejudices instead of admitting truths and seeking extenuating suggestions to cushion the effects of hard facts. The stable democracies never distort facts in their national politics to suit the prejudices of any group. The only manifest fact that people are unable to distort is poverty. If Ghanaians continue to refrain from being candid, the better Ghana will elude us, and we shall be thrown into labyrinthine darkness. The better attitude is to concede truth and avoid posthumous sycophancy or fanaticism.

There were undesirable totalitarian and tyrannical suppressions in Ghana from 1958, climaxing in a "dawn broadcast" of 1962 by then president Nkrumah, which derogated from encouraging economic and financial prosperity and well-being that normally result from hard work, enterprise, and organization. For this reason, any political groupings today claiming to be absolute followers of Nkrumah's footsteps must also be courageous to concede the flaws in his governance. There should be no perversion of logic to justify mischief. Only the desirable tenets of previous leaders deserve emulation.

The charismatic involvement of the massive common citizenry that distinguished Nkrumah's Convention People's Party (CPP) from the method of Danquah's United Gold Coast Conversion (UGCC) in 1948 was laudable, but what eluded Ghanaians was freedom. After the capture of political leadership by the CPP under Nkrumah, there was the refusal (call it failure) of the CPP leadership to liberalize the society after independence for Ghanaians to enjoy the real freedom they were promised in counterpoint to colonial domination. Ghanaians were rather subjected to a regime of tyrannical dictatorship until 1966. In this context, therefore, the new CPP leadership seeking to emulate the yesteryear CPP must convince Ghanaians by renouncing the obvious flaws in governance during the period between 1958 and 1966. Otherwise, it will be taken that, then, to the new CPP leadership, those flaws were proper and justified and should be repeated after ratification. The other alternative stance would be to deny that there were flaws. All these border on intellectual honesty. Unbridled sycophancy or inordinate fanaticism cannot promote a healthy society. Neither should ethnic bigotry dominate governance.

For they necessarily distort the facts to the new generations in educating those who never knew or saw the nature of the avoidable things that took place from 1958 until the spate of all the military takeovers.

The Involvement of the Masses

Dr. Danquah's political flaw might be that he was too much reserved in his leadership style, but he had never been known to be a separatist or a federalist. J. B. Danquah was a misunderstood leader whose patriotic vision remained nebulous to most Ghanaians, so it is quite unfair to him to associate him with Busia's politics. There was no government led by J. B. Danquah as known to the people of Ghana because the UGCC, which J. B. Danquah led, had been neutralized in 1948, and it fizzled out of political reckoning by 1949. K. A. Busia was politically unknown prior to 1954 when he formed and led the Ghana Congress Party (GCP). Busia had been a colonial servant styled as a district commissioner prior to 1954. J. B. Danquah failed to win a parliamentary seat in 1954 as an independent candidate. He never stood on the ticket of any party, let alone K. A. Busia's GCP. Although J. B. Danquah propounded the name Ghana for this country, he and Busia were never one in their visions for Ghana. They would have belonged to the same political party by 1954. Therefore, there was no known desideratum shared by Danquah and Busia as a common political purpose or method since Dr. Danquah's UGCC had fizzled out five clear years before Dr. Busia's GCP was formed. The so-called accolade, which goes by "Danquah-Busia tradition," is thus a false and misleading slogan, which is unfair to Danquah.

The truth is that there was Busia-Dombo politics of separation. What is however true is that at different times, like many other persons, both Dr. Danquah and Dr. Busia foresaw and sought to resist the tyrannical proclivity in Nkrumah as a person. Moreover, when Nkrumah and the others broke away from the UGCC and formed the CPP, Nkrumah's charisma and popularity soared, owing largely to the able personalities who joined him, such as K. A. Gbedemah, C. T. Nylander, N. A. Welbeck, Archie Casely-Hayford, Kojo Botsio, E. Ako-Adjei, E. O. Asafu Adjaye, L. R. Abavana, J. H. Allasani, Mumuni Bawumia, J. E. Jantua, J. E. Hagan, Imoru Egala, etc. (almost all of them broke away from the UGCC). They remained together united in the common purpose to (as they put it) "join the colony with Ashanti, Togoland with Northern Territories and then we manage our own affairs." Indeed, this was the original nation-building plan of the UGCC by 1948. These leaders remained united in the CPP with a common agenda of making a unitary state of Ghana out of the various heterogeneous ethnic groups dear to their hearts even when Nkrumah was in prison. They and many more others really actually nurtured and fostered the Ghanaian nation, not Nkrumah. Nkrumah alone could never have done that. This is what ought to be conceded and recognized and not the continuation of posthumous sycophancy or fanaticism as a weakness, which led to the collapse of the first republic.

In the struggle for independence, Ghanaians saw, apart from CPP, many political groups in the names of Ghana Congress Party (GCP), whose name sounded ideal and appealed to many of the youth, including this humble writer, led by K. A. Busia, but which could not permeate the whole Gold Coast as a political party. The others were Anlo Youth Organization (AYO); Muslim Youth Association (MYA); Togo Congress Party (TCP), which was better called Ablode; Northern People's Party (NPP); and National Liberation Movement (NLM), whose slogan was "Mate meho." But they were all tribally and locally centered. And there was an uprising—a purely local and tribal group that arose in Accra, calling itself Ga Shifimo Kpee, which has "Gboi ngbe wo" (Strangers are killing us) as its slogan.

The Need for Vital Absence of Inordinate Ethnicism

As all the foregoing groups preached federalism and separation of some sorts, they were noted as opposing the CPP, and they failed to unite because of their stance in the independence struggle. Surely if they, those separatist groups, had succeeded in their desires and methods against the CPP, there could not have been Ghana as we have it today. Moreover, it was only out of desperation that those groups came together as a nominal "united party" after independence and only after the Preventive Detention Act (PDA) had unnecessarily crippled them, although the electorate in 1956, the UN plebiscite of that year, had rubbed out their separatist colour.

Busia's political clout and influence and effort in governance in Ghana came up in the post–military coup activities in 1966–1967 in which he participated and later led. Candidly, the military coup, which terminated Nkrumah's CPP rule in 1966,[3] was inevitable and supportable, although the performance of the National Liberation Council (NLC) military cum police junta whose political adviser was Busia was a disaster.

The mother of all the military takeovers subsequent to the 1966 coup was Busia's influence, method, policy, and regime spanning 1967–1972. While each military regime between 1972 and 1992 stands each in its unique stance for analysis and assessment regarding justification and excesses, the new CPP leaders are enjoined to show themselves for all to see that they are

---

3   That government was not representative. There were no elections. The CPP leadership only picked any person to go to parliament (1964/65).

intellectually honest. The NPP, too, must openly identify the flaws of the erstwhile PP/NLC government/regimes during the period spanning 1967–1972 and renounce those flaws. The failure to do so suggests that they cannot claim any honest leadership that will uphold what will enhance the well-being of the electorate.

They must eschew identified mischiefs of the past involving the regimes whose footsteps they profess to follow and not to wantonly and exclusively continue to appropriate to themselves state properties. The electorate have, however, jettisoned that trend by the results of the 2008 elections. People only resort to wholesale slogans purporting to claim that they are emulating a previous group. By so doing, they profess to justify all the flaws of those governments. Today in Ghana, there is no political party that has the military as its base. There is therefore no need to belabour pre-1992 excesses of the revolutionary military regimes or keep those excesses in mind for acting in certain ways. The conscious electorates need to sieve issues in their quiet.

Political parties therefore need openness in educating the new generation of the electorate to know and become conscious of what happened in the past and what is desirable for Ghana at all times. To be able to sieve the flaws or mischiefs of the past and eschew them to be able to emulate the desirables, there must be honest identification of the flaws of the past and conscientious efforts and professing.

The vital question is, What is desirable for the people of Ghana? Is it the grandiose lifestyle of the leaders or moderation in our society? The country belongs to us; we are taking the country, or we all belong to Ghana no matter where one comes from in Ghana.

Those whose notion had been "Oman no ye yen dea, ye gye yen man" (The country belongs to us, we are taking our country) must drop that notion now and forever because it is vain as it is bigotry. Ghana belongs to all Ghanaians, and every Ghanaian belongs to Ghana. There is actually no use for anything that derogates from conceding truths and accepting facts. This calls for acknowledgment and recognition of all who made worthy contribution to the making of our linguistically international island nation of Ghana from scratch.

We learned about the Gold Coast Aboriginal Society before the two world wars. However, the real serious struggle for the making of the Ghanaian nation began after the Second World War. It was led by Dr. J. B. Danquah with Pa Grant, the highly successful merchant, as the major financier. Dr. J. B. Danquah propounded the name Ghana for the nation to be made out of all the territories under the colonial power of Britain called the Gold Coast and Togoland, culminating in the 1956 plebiscite. Any attempt to reverse this will be catastrophic. Ghanaians have made the Ghanaian nation.

Positive Action

Ghana's independence struggle gained real momentum after the 1948 disturbances, which followed the famous declaration of "positive action" that year. However, many people have not really fully appreciated the substance of that declaration. Yet still there is often no discussion of the event of 1948 without mentioning the declaration of "positive action."

The first problem of most people is that it has never been clear to them who declared the "positive action" and what it did mean. There is also a cloud surrounding whether the "positive action" was declared against the colonial administration. Very few people can sincerely deny that the United Gold Coast Convention (UGCC) was the nationalist movement that laid the foundation that brought into being the Ghanaian nation as we have it today.

The UGCC membership was open to all citizens of the Gold Coast and never restricted. What used to be called the Gold Coast is now Ghana, comprising what was known as the colony, i.e., all the southern provinces of Eastern, Central, Greater Accra, and Western Regions; Ashanti including Brong-Ahafo Region and the Northern Territories, which are now the Northern, Upper East, and Upper West Regions; and the Trusteeship Togoland, which is now part of the Volta Region. However, the leadership of the UGCC was made up of few very highly educated natives and intellectuals—mainly lawyers, teachers, merchants, and tribal chiefs—to give support. At the apex of the UGCC leadership was Dr. J. B. Danquah with university graduates and professionals.

The aim and plans of the UGCC were to put together all the aforementioned areas then called colonial territories as a sovereign nation to shed the colonial yoke as we have it today. But the other ranks of the UGCC and the chiefs in particular became dissatisfied with some perceived organizational shortcomings in the movement's leadership, which gave them cause to grumble. They perceived that the leadership had no respect for the intelligence of the other ranks of the movement and the chiefs. For example, Dr. J. B. Danquah did not find it necessary to condescend to the level of the common people, so he did not find it necessary to travel on the same plane with the tribal chiefs he led to a constitutional conference in London. The UGCC leadership did not find any of the ranking members of the movement fit for appointment as general secretary, except a lawyer or a university graduate or a holder of a professional qualification of a sort. So that when E. Ako-Adjei, a very busy lawyer, was proposed for the job, he declined with the excuse that he would not be able to combine his busy legal practice with the post of general secretary of the UGCC. He therefore had to suggest Kwame Nkrumah, whom he knew in London, as a very able man for the job.

Having become convinced, the UGCC leadership remitted £100 to Nkrumah in London for him to travel from London by ship via Liverpool to Takoradi and to take up the job of general secretary of the UGCC. Nkrumah had two master's degrees from two American universities, but he had no professional qualification, so it was assumed that he would have no divided attention. He would be able to devote his full time to the position of general secretary of the movement.

The UGCC leadership, however, blundered from the scratch. They failed to make any arrangement for accommodation for Nkrumah as general secretary. He therefore had to put a mattress on the *floor*[4] of one of the rooms of the premises housing the headquarters of the UGCC. However, as providence would have it, one of the active members of the UGCC, K. A. Gbedemah, having seen Nkrumah, recognized that he was a student he knew from the Achimota Training College by the name Francis Kofi Nwiah at the time he (Gbedemah) and Willie Ofori Attah also were in the Achimota Secondary School as classmates. Dissatisfied with Nkrumah's plight as UGCC general secretary, Gbedemah daftly took him to his home at Farrah Avenue, Adabraka, to share his home with him in 1947. Therefore, Nkrumah remained with Gbedemah as Gbedemah's guest until Nkrumah became leader of government business in 1951 when a donor gave Nkrumah an accommodation in Accra New Town, formerly called Lagos Town. If this were by way of parenthesis, it would however point to the attitude of the UGCC leadership toward the other ranks of their movement.

Almost as a matter of cause, there arose serious disagreements between Nkrumah and the leadership of the UGCC, leading to consequential neutralization of the movement itself and an eventual formation of the Convention People's Party (CPP).

The UGCC leadership had made two proposals—one to Nkrumah and the other to K. A. Gbedemah—which both men rejected. The two proposals looked offensive and naive at the same time. In the first place, Nkrumah was told by his employers, the UGCC leadership, to accept another donation of £100 to enable him to go back to Britain and carry on with his studies there toward becoming a lawyer. K. A. Gbedemah was now offered the position of general secretary of the UGCC in place of Nkrumah, who had been his guest all this time; hence, both men obviously rejected the two offers. It is not clear to this writer whether Nkrumah wisely took the £100 and refused to go back to Britain or rejected the money with the proposal, which he considered an insult to him. K. A. Gbedemah had all the time been an active member of the UGCC with

---

4   Kwame Nkrumah, *The Autobiography of Kwame Nkrumah* (Legon: African Writers Series, Balm Library, University of Ghana).

his acknowledged highly intellectual ability, yet the movement's leadership did not find him fit to be general secretary until after his friend and guest was sacked from the same job.

Meanwhile, the other ranks of the UGCC members had had the perception that the leadership of the movement was not being dynamic and was not doing well enough toward implementing the plan of the movement in putting together the various groups toward shedding the colonial yoke to make a sovereign nation out of the various heterogeneous areas under the colonial authority. So at one UGCC rally in Accra in 1948, one of the ranking members of the UGCC called Dzenkle Jewu declared that there was to be, from that day, positive action toward realizing the aspirations of the UGCC and not to be obsessed with who should be general secretary. Clearly, therefore, the declaration of the positive action was by Dzenkle Jewu against the leadership of the UGCC and not Kwame Nkrumah against the colonial administration. However, the declaration was misconstrued and hijacked by the masses who mistook it to be a declaration for lawlessness and looting rather than a declaration for urging their leaders to act with dynamism toward realizing the movement's aspirations.

Inculcation of Truly National Consciousness

The colonial authorities took offence and decided to arrest those responsible for the disturbances and the looting. The UGCC leadership erroneously shifted the blame onto Nkrumah, but the colonial authorities could not get him readily. They therefore went for his host, K. A. Gbedemah. When they succeeded in arresting Nkrumah eventually, Gbedemah was released from prison. Clearly it was the refusal of K. A. Gbedemah to be general secretary of the UGCC in place of Nkrumah in 1948 that effectively neutralized the UGCC and finally sank that movement into permanent oblivion. Just at that juncture, the dissatisfied UGCC members and some other persons came together and formed the Convention People's Party (CPP), and Nkrumah was declared as their leader. Nkrumah then consciously started taking successful steps to forestall any rivalry to his fortuitous leadership of the CPP. The result was eventually the breeding of hordes of inordinate fanatics and sycophants countrywide. With the UGCC having thus been sunk into and remained in oblivion since then and with the arrest of Nkrumah and the simultaneous release from prison of Gbedemah, the CPP fell under the leadership of K. A. Gbedemah, who spearheaded the independence struggle throughout the Gold Coast in collaboration with other faithful supporters carrying the original UGCC message, which now became adopted by the CPP: "Our aim and purpose are to put together the colony and Ashanti, Togoland and the Northern Territories and then to manage our own affairs and shed the colonial yoke." The colonial administration eventually agreed that there should be a general election in 1951. The CPP leadership insisted that Nkrumah should be allowed to stand as a candidate in the election, being convinced that if he should win. Nkrumah would be released from prison, and any legal proceedings in court for his release would be unnecessary and stalled. Yet when the news was broken to Nkrumah in the prison by Gbedemah, there was a paradox as Nkrumah refused to stand in an election in his hometown and insisted that he would stand in Accra Central, where Gbedemah had registered as a candidate having lived in Accra for decades and taught science at Accra Academy and married from *Central*[5] Accra.

This being the first clash between the two, it was resolved with Gbedemah agreeing to move to Keta, his native town where he had not visited for decades. Both men won their seats overwhelmingly. On his release from prison, Nkrumah was made leader of government business by the governor in 1951, and Gbedemah became minister of commerce and industry. Nkrumah and Gbedemah had other known interesting clashes. One was over the insistence of Nkrumah, who then became prime minister, that his effigy must be on the currency of the country on attaining independence in 1957, over which Gbedemah resigned as the minister of finance. But their differences were later composed by compromises. Their other and final known clash was over ideology in 1962, which sent Gbedemah into exile, and Nkrumah did an unthinkable mischief against Gbedemah. Nkrumah, still fearing that Gbedemah was a threat to his power in Ghana, stooped very low and printed a falsehood in millions of copies, which he caused to be distributed all over the world, that Gbedemah had stolen

---

5   Parliamentary Hansards (1951–1960 editions).

Ghana's £10 million. When his close associates that time asked him about the propriety of that false publication, all that Nkrumah said was, "These things happen in politics." It is hereby supposed that this was a most callous and most reprehensible thing to do in politics with public fund. Nkrumah's tyranny had then reached its peak.

Viewing this alongside the lies being peddled and the mischiefs being contemplated by some people in the Ghanaian political terrain, one becomes sick and worried. Such a thing should be condemned and never to be emulated in the Ghanaian public life. It should be eschewed completely. Therefore, when people sing the praises of past leaders, we should never lose sight of their mischiefs too. No one's suffering or unjustifiable death is to be cherished or welcomed. To be intellectually honest to sing praise where praise is due, condemn mischief and eschew them completely no matter where they are found and who committed them, lest we deviate from the worthy democratic path.

Politics can still be without such condemnable and depraved behaviours in trying to win and retain power at all cost. There is hereby a call for facultative revolution in the politics of Africa, which is to jettison mischiefs and mischievous ideas or plans and replace them with patriotism properly so understood.

1. That government was not representative. There were no elections. The CPP leadership only picked any person to go to parliament (1964/65).
2. The enactment of the Preventive Detention Act (PDA) and its abuses.
3. *Autobiography of Kwame Nkrumah* (Legon: African Writers Series, Balm Library, University of Ghana).
4. Parliamentary Hansards (1951–1960 editions).

CHAPTER THREE

THE NIGERIAN PROBLEM—ITS ORIGIN AND CONSTITUTIONAL ARRANGEMENT IN THE FEDERAL REPUBLIC OF NIGERIA (1951–1954)

The appointment of a British consul in Nigeria in 1849 has been noted in contrast to a bond made between the lieutenant governor and eight coastal chiefs of the Gold Coast Colony in 1844. But in Nigeria, the appointment of the consul was rapidly followed by other official actions in the form of changes, fighting, annexations, and mergers and, in some cases, redelineation of boundaries of territorial authority, so much so that within a period of fifty years, all the territories of Southern and Northern Nigeria were declared British Protectorates in 1900 and merged with Lagos in 1906. By 1914, all the Southern and Northern Protectorates were amalgamated. A governor-general was appointed with legislative powers to make laws. Some natives were also appointed for consultation through them with local opinion before legislation. That might probably qualify to be the first constitutional arrangement for how Nigeria would be governed by Britain. But it was only under the 1922 arrangement that the first elective principle was introduced.

A legislative council comprising forty-six members with four elected from Lagos and Calabar was created. The forty-six elected members were to sit with the governor who presided and twenty-three official members. Fifteen other unofficial members were nominated under what is now popularly referred to as the Clifford Constitution.

In 1946, the Richards Constitutional Arrangement replaced the Clifford Arrangement. It saw the first unofficial majority on the Legislative Council. Under this constitutional arrangement, the Legislative Council also had power to enact laws for the whole country. The regional councils were to act as advisory bodies, and they had no legislative powers whatsoever. Property qualification for voting and to be voted for was retained. In the two southern regions of East and West, there were single Houses of Assembly, while the North had both a House of Assembly and a House of Chiefs. Dr. Elias thinks that the 1946 Richards Constitutional Arrangement made an advanced effort in the direction of representative government in Nigeria. He is of the view that the arrangement broadened the selection and the basis of Nigerian participation in the *legislative process*[6] . However, it would appear that the 1946 arrangement still failed to break the North-South dichotomy and exacerbated it by creating two regional advisory bodies in the North alone and one each in the Eastern and Western Regions.

That arrangement did not also show any basis for creating the Northern Region that was almost three times the size of the East and the West put together, except on the grounds of (the Islamic) religion, because in the North, just as the South, the people are not homogenous. Apart from the Northeastern Zone, the Middle Belt was not in any way a justifiable part of the North. Moreover, the Niger and the Benue Rivers clearly formed natural boundary demarcations, but the colonial authorities failed to take these into consideration. Thus, the anomalous imbalance was further carried in the 1951 constitutional arrangement.

Under the 1951 McPherson Constitutional Arrangement, the so-called North was left so large that it looked on the map like a huge octopus about to swallow all the other regions of the South put together.

---

6   Legislative process.

Although a House of Representatives was created at the centre, the regions remained uneven. The North alone as one region sent sixty-eight members into the House of Representatives, while the East and the West sent thirty-four members each to equal the Northern number in the 136 elected members to the House of Representatives. Again, each region had a regional assembly. But the North and the West had additional Houses of Chiefs. Under the McPherson Constitution, the legislative power in Nigeria was vested in the governor, who wielded the power to bring into force any bill that was not passed by the House of Representatives.

There was a central Council of Ministers comprising four ministers from each region's House of Assembly selected by the governor on the recommendation of the lieutenant governor. There were no direct elections into the various assemblies and to the House of Representatives. Although, the 1951 arrangement in Nigeria, too, saw the abolition of property qualifications, the indirect election of members of the various assemblies through electoral colleges provided opportunities for political mischief making in the form of carpet crossing based on ethnic consideration. This was the situation because the Regional Assemblies acting as electoral colleges elected the regional members of the House of Representatives and also because the leader of government in the Regional Assembly was also similarly elected by an electoral college of the House. Furthermore, twelve years of residential qualification was introduced to replace the hitherto property ownership qualification.

What is quite apparent, and ought to have been realized by the African leadership in Nigeria at the time, was that all the previous constitutional arrangements, including that of 1951, showed that those who controlled power and influence in Britain at the time had never been and were not keen about issues that could make Nigeria a cohesive and close-knit federation. In this connection, some sections of the Nigerian leadership itself cannot escape culpability in their parochial and self-centered agitations based on ethnicity, tribal bias, and religious prejudice. These traits, much unfortunately, are those same ones that bedevil and haunt the Nigerian federation to the present day. Ironically, those sentiments did succeed to strengthen and propel the British agenda but weaken and negate the evolution of a cohesive federated Nigeria.

CHAPTER FOUR

CONSTITUTIONAL ARRANGEMENTS IN THE FEDERATION OF NIGERIA (1951–1954)

The constitutional arrangement for Nigeria in 1954 created three regions, namely, Northern Region, Western Region, and Eastern Region and a virtual fourth region that was Southern Cameroon. Again, this time, it was not deemed—perhaps not desired—that there should emerge in West Africa a nation of Nigeria that was cohesive, stable, and viable. Perhaps, too, there was no desirability on the part of those who mattered to consciously craft a nation out of the heterogeneous tribal units of the North, West, and East of Nigeria.

The Federal Constitution provided for a federal legislature in 1954—a House of Representatives comprising 184 members elected by direct and free franchise. But the arrangements were such that the North alone was left intact as one region, sending more than twice the representation of all the southern regions put together to the Federal House of Representatives.

Meanwhile, the Cameroonians had been examining the sensibility and rationality of joining Nigeria at independence in a most difficult type of federation. From the indeterminate and irresolute attitude of the British colonialists to the outstanding issues begging for address and redress in Nigeria and other emerging nations, it is quite clearly evident that at this juncture, the colonialists did not have any clear-cut pattern of policy or standard for the states or entities being forced by the tide of history to be created in the African continent. For until Nigeria became independent in 1960, Southern Cameroon was administered by Britain as part of Nigeria. French Cameroon (Northern Cameroon) was proclaimed independent on January 1, 1960. One would have therefore thought that independence would be granted to a people being administered together by the same colonial power at the same time since the United Nations Trusteeship Commission Report[7*] had stated that the Cameroons (South and North) were separate entities and different people put together. In view of this, it could not be said that the south or British Cameroon must be made to join its kinsfolk of the Republic of Cameroon because they are different people. Hence, to conceive the idea of a plebiscite in Southern (British) Cameroon was rather strange and uncalled for. No doubt, many African states abstained from voting on the resolution after a protracted debate of the issue at the United Nations.[8]

It is submitted that the decision to hold a plebiscite in French (Northern) Cameroon was in order, but the questions posed that were to be answered by the plebiscite were wrong and not in order; they were abnormal. The question for Northern Cameroon ought to have been whether the North should join Nigeria on independence and not whether it should go with Northern Nigeria. Northern Nigeria was not being considered for independence separate from the rest of Nigeria. However, if that was what the British authorities contemplated, it was never made known. Again, it ought to have been asked whether the country (Southern Cameroon) should join Nigeria as part of that federation or remain on their own and not whether their future should be determined on a later date. In both cases, the questions were framed to avoid asking the two Cameroons whether they would rather prefer to unite on their own or join Nigeria.

7　* The UN Information Centre, Lagos, Accra.
8　The UN Information Centre, Lagos, Accra.

It was quite clear that the possibility of Cameroon as a whole joining Nigeria at independence was what the colonial powers did not want to see happen. And when the political difficulties being created by the Nigerian leadership itself at the efforts being made toward Nigerian nationhood had been made apparent, the neutral powers and progressive elements who had influence with the colonial powers had no sympathy or admiration for the internal arrangements in Nigeria. So the questions for the plebiscite were framed in such a way that Cameroon must necessarily find a more plausible and attractive alternative other than to join Nigeria. If Cameroon had joined Nigeria at independence, the years-old feud between the two neighbour countries over the Bakassi Peninsula, which was grudgingly settled only in 2007, would have been obviated.

The 1954 Constitution was the arrangement under which Nigeria attained independence from British colonial rule. In 1963, however, Nigeria was declared a republic. Yet no effort was made to address the North-South imbalance in the scheme of things, save that a Midwestern Region was carved out of Western Region, and Nigeria's problem of unity and cohesion still lingered on.

It would require a facultative revolution, thorough and radical in nature, to evolve and implement urgent and necessary action backed by law, to knit the inhabitants of that area of the continent known as Nigeria together into what can be truly described as one country or one nation or one federation. As at present, the matrix is lacking or absent.

Patriotism, Nationalism, and Statesmanship

One is bound sometimes to attempt an examination of the meaning of certain abstract terms. Words like *love*, *patriotism*, *nationalism*, and statesmanship tend to present difficulties in defining their meanings since they intertwine conceptually.

Patriotism has been defined as the acts and conduct of a person actuated by the love of his country. It is a demonstration of this through one's conduct

24

and actions directed toward enhancing the general public welfare. A patriot is therefore a person who strongly supports his country.

Nationalism is said to be a strong devotion to one's country. It also connotes patriotic feelings, devotions, efforts, and principles. The term has become more associated with a movement for political and social independence in a country controlled by a colonial power or any other country from outside. A nationalist is therefore a supporter of nationalism.

Statesmanship is the skill and the wisdom in managing public affairs. A statesman is said to be a person who takes an important part in the management of state affairs. A statesman is known to be a disinterested political leader who is broad-minded in his outlook when considering matters of the nation.

Love has always been preached at various gatherings, even on political party platforms by people canvassing for votes. *Love* fundamentally connotes warmth and kind feeling, fondness and affection, concern and devotion. But love has several shades that can be demonstrated in equally different ways. There is a mother's love and tender affection for her children. There is love for studies and love for adventure. There is a person's love for his or her parents and love for a spouse. These attitudes are all capable of demonstration in different ways. Yet there is an element of love in being patriotic, in being nationalistic, and in being statesmanlike. So that for anybody's conduct to be deemed to have the animation of any of these, the one must have displayed some element of love. But this is sometimes abstruse. It is not easy to decide whether or not people who organize and execute coups d'état to topple the government of their country and kill in the process can be called true patriots or nationalists or at all statesmen because they have succeeded. Such people are, however, readily condemned when they have failed in their bid to topple the government. Thus, it seems the Bible can be misconstrued, if not misleading, in certain, of its teachings because some of its provisions are very deep in meaning and sometimes abstruse. For the Bible does not support a determined effort to eliminate a person who is knowingly determined to kill or otherwise destroy another. The Bible will support only a defensive position that is always the weaker position. And to what is agreed on earth is also agreed in heaven—a stance that ultimately suggests like Machiavelli that the end justifies the means.

The foregoing only serves to illustrate certain difficulties that are entailed in matters pertaining to human life and concepts. Yet still patriotism is only an abstract term that can be demonstrated only through certain overt acts. A patriot can also be a nationalist and a statesman. It follows, therefore, that at everyone's level of interaction in the society, one can be patriotic or otherwise. One does not have to wait until one's country is at war before one shows one's patriotic zeal by demonstrating the truly ostentatious and injudicious love for one's country or nation. It is demonstrable anytime anywhere at any level. But it is not in foolhardiness.

However, patriotism in Africa is bound to be contextually more complex and not easy to ascertain. The reason is basically found in the heterogeneity of African societies, which poses a problem of identifying one's nation and one's people. Underpinning this problem is the absence of the patriotic willingness to make a nation stretching beyond one's ethnic and parochial confines of religion or tribe or by whatever way it is determined. The first practically patriotic step is the identification of one's fatherland. That is to say, the identification of the nation recognized by an individual as his own. Because our nation building is still going on, our patriotic vision is to be found in our demonstration to build a nation that we can call our own, and our patriotic efforts should therefore be directed that way and measured that way. The patriotic vision is narrow and myopic when it is based on religion and ethnicity. This is highly undesirable because it denies the African people a reasonable chance to build nations viable enough for a takeoff economically and socially by pulling resources together. It has distorted and continues to distort the natural growth of the African nations by disturbing the process of social evolution generated by nationalism in the continent. It has succeeded in suppressing the chance of creating and fostering the atmosphere needed for enhancing Africa's social conditions, which will augment the people's material well-being. The cumulative result is the denial to Africa reasonable viability to compete favorably among the comity of nations in the industrial and other social and economic spheres.

There is no denying the point as a valid contention though that because there were no nations properly so-called other than the ethnic and tribal groups, one was bound initially, first and foremost, to belong to one's ethnic or tribal or other known identities and therefore one's patriotic vision should properly be found therein.

While there is no denial of this here and now, the better contention is that nation building must necessarily start from some base by all means. However, the tribal and ethnic groups having been subsumed under one colonial administration in one case and the same ethnic or tribal entity in other cases having been wrongly separated, there was provided a wider and more viable basis for founding a nation that, in modern terms, must have been more worthwhile. And an attempt to thwart efforts to so build that nation or make the building of it extremely difficult or impossible by capitalizing on tribe and ethnicity or religion was not a demonstration of patriotic vision. If the prevention was the result of lack of appreciation of the greater benefit and satisfaction derivable from building the nation on the wider basis, then the leadership preventing it must be incompetent. If the leadership preventing the development of wider basis into a nation was actuated by the fact that the leadership of the nation on wider basis inevitably would fall on anyone other than himself or his tribesman, then there was absolute absence of patriotic qualities in that showing. Thus, on the evaluation of the evidence in the Nigerian context, no favorable verdict can go to Ahmadu Bello and Obafemi Awolowo on the bases of the foregoing. Awolowo was a tribal leader who did not regard as his people others outside his tribe, and Ahmadu Bello was a religious bigot who did not consider non-Muslims as his people. Both were too much obsessed with only the interests of their respective sections and not Nigeria as a whole. They were not interested in having Nigeria as we have it today, and as we wish still to have it in the morrow, in any case, both could hardly qualify as statesmen.

Altruism and Patriotism

Statesmanship, nationalism, and patriotism, we have seen, have a common feature, which is a disinterested love for one's nation. Their definitions and meanings, too, are intertwined and correlated. It is intended to examine presently the validity of or the extent to which it can be validly said that patriotism or statesmanship is altruistic. The statesman or patriot or the nationalist belongs to the nation he regards or recognizes as his own. If he was born into the nation already existing, he recognizes it as his fatherland or motherland. He belongs to the nation, and the people of that nation are his people. If, as is often the case with young nations, a people have been under any foreign domination of any kind or a colony fighting for self-determination, he belongs to a people fighting to make a nation. In each case, it is submitted that a statesman's interest is inclusive. He cannot be said to be disinterested in what he is doing because he has interest in the welfare of his people. Therefore, the acts of a patriot in promoting the welfare of his people cannot be properly described as altruistic in the absolute sense of the word. But it will be equally wrong and perhaps more wrong to say that self-interest is the motivating factor of all patriotic acts.

A patriot provides leadership and gets paid for it a fee or salary. However, it cannot be said that he is motivated solely by the fee or salary that he earns to seek to lead his people. In many cases, leadership is provided by patriots who, in monetary terms, descend from bigger incomes to serve their nations. Another interest may be the good name or reputation that a patriot may earn by good leadership. He may possibly become notorious or hated, too, by others. But all this forms the concomitant incidence of leadership and patriotism, and it will be unfair to say that self-interest motivates it.

Self-interest is not a neutral term. It connotes the egoistic theory that everyone's action is always caused by one's desire to benefit oneself. The fact is that to say that a patriot or statesman himself necessarily benefits also from his patriotic acts is a truism. An analogy between patriotism and decision to get married may be drawn and made completely devoid of perversion. While sexual intercourse between spouses is an incidence of marriage, it will be perverse to say that people who decide to get married do so purely and only because of sexual connection. This is not so. Several other factors motivate different people's decision to get married at all. Some spouses continue to live together without sex or even childbearing. This shows that because a thing inevitably results from certain actions does not suggest that the action is motivated purely because of the result where that is not the only possible result of that act. The benefits derivable from the act of a patriot are inclusive. It cannot, however, be said that one's patriotic act is motivated purely by those benefits where the benefits are not exclusive to him to the utter detriment of all others except the honour.

Another important factor that is always ignored or that many people do not appreciate is that patriotism implies the satisfaction of the patriot for good and noble acts. A true patriot must really feel satisfied by the good results of his patriotic conduct, without which there cannot be any motivator at all. Without motivation, there cannot be any action. Where the motivation is corrupt and perverse, it is unpatriotic. Where it is laudable, it is also patriotic, and it will be an abnormal person—in fact, a deviant—who will not wish to feel satisfied by the worthy results of his good and patriotic acts. If by this it has been shown that absolute disinterestedness will be incompatible with patriotism, that is the aim. Thus, to deny a person praises where they are due to him on the ground that his actions were meant to satisfy himself is deviant if that satisfaction is desired for good and patriotic work. We have been contending that altruism in its absolute sense cannot be compatible with patriotism or nationalism, because by being disinterested, there will be the absence of conviction and conscientiousness. This will necessarily culminate into perfunctory acts. Yet no stretch of any imagination can ever convert a perfunctory act into a patriotic act.

Therefore, a disinterested person in any cause cannot be a patriotic person, nor can he ever graduate to the higher status of a statesman. We have so far been thinking in terms of political and other similar social actions that lie on different plains from purely technical or professional acts of a publicly spirited person acting according to the dictates of his conscience toward his less fortunate fellows. An example is a medical doctor who is not bound in any way to treat a patient suffering from a communicable disease but chooses to do so and, in the process, contracts the disease himself. Another example may be found in a person who believes he can dive and swim and plunges into a river in an attempt to rescue a drowning friend or any person. These two examples are manifestly different from a political leadership situation. The attitudes and considerations are clearly different, and in such situations, the person—the doctor who becomes affected by the disease he cures or the diver who gets drowned—can be said to have acted in a disinterested manner and therefore altruistically. Otherwise, all patriotic acts of a patriot or a statesman or nationalist have all the benefits inclusive, i.e., the actor's interest is and must be involved. In the case of the doctor or the diver's act, the victim's life is saved for the sake of saving. We have been demonstrating by argument that while the terms *patriot*, *statesman*, and *nationalist* can be synonymous, a *philanthropist* is not a synonym of any of them, although all the four are of the same generic terms. Only a philanthropist can properly be expected to act in a disinterested manner, and in that respect, or because of that, it is sui generis, while the rest can be ejusdem generis. All this is to demonstrate that there are different shades in which generic terms can be conceptualized.

Many black Africans tend to hide behind their ethnic prejudices to denigrate their fellow African patriots on the ground that their actions were motivated by self-interest and not altruism. They do so only to satisfy a craving to deny praise where praise is due. This tendency in itself is unpatriotic since patriotism is furthered by giving support to patriotic acts whether the support is concrete or moral or material or all these three. However, patriotism is not the same thing as bigotry. A bigot holds his views and refuses to rub his mind with other people. He holds onto his views strongly and refuses to accept reason or argument. Nor is a demagogue necessarily a patriot, or at all, in certain cases, demagogy and bigotry are fused in one personality and a tyranny is born.

Patriotism is not clannishness. Therefore, it is often a wrong tendency to distort the virtues of patriotism. To be clannish is to show clan feeling. Clannishness is therefore the habit of showing clan feeling by supporting one another against people who do not belong to the same clan. Clannishness, in this context, includes nepotism, which is the giving of special favours to relations by a person in high position.

The relations meant here must not be restricted to blood relations alone. Relations include religious associates, club members and members of the same societies, and alumni of educational institutions. When clannishness has as its paramount influential factor language and custom on racial basis, then it is tribally based. Clannishness therefore encompasses parochialism and tribalism. A reference to any particular cultural group exclusively is clannishness based on ethnicity. The manifestations of the influences of foregoing forms of clannishness in some African countries are very alarming. In certain cases, it is effrontery on a very high scale, but in other cases, it is foolhardy and rather disgraceful. The issue is not that one should not have any clan feelings at all. The protest is against the insistence that clannishness cannot be a nonissue. No one can sanely complain against a private trader helping his friend in any way in private business. But even then, if the capability to help is there, to decline to do so purely on the basis of clan or to be enthusiastic to do so on the same basis must be frowned upon because it is retrograde. The personal quality aspect must be paramount and preferred. Africans can enjoy prosperous and better standard of living in larger communities. Better quality of life can be realized in Africa if attitudes transcend clannish inhibitions. Extremely absurd exhibition of inimical clannishness is capable of threatening the sovereignty of even the existing states in Africa. When rival football clubs of the same country vie for the country's championship trophy, one must always win when the others naturally lose.

Let us take practical cases here. Accra Hearts of Oak and Asante Kotoko football clubs are two rival clubs in Ghana. In 1980/81 football season, Kotoko qualified for the continental competition for the cup winner's trophy, but they crashed out very early in that competition that season. Hearts of Oak qualified for the continental competition for the champion club trophy and worked hard to reach the final, which was played in Cameroon between Vita Club of Cameroon and Hearts of Oak of Ghana, which could be fairly said that the referee gave the trophy to the Cameroonian club. It was so disheartening to observe that the Asante Kotoko supporters were effronterically supporting the Cameroonians club against Hearts of Oak as they listened in to Radio Ghana's commentary in Accra to the extent that when a controversial penalty was awarded to the Cameroonians and the most enterprising and versatile player of Hearts that day was sent off the field for daring to question the referee's award of the penalty, some supporters of Kotoko openly jubilated even though their club was not involved. They were not in agreement that Hearts of Oak, too, should go on record as having won the African championship. They wanted only Kotoko to remain the Ghanaian club that succeeded ever to win that trophy. In that kind of situation, the attitude of the Asante Kotoko supporters was not only unpatriotic but also extremely malicious. The same result would be true if the Cameroonians opponents of Vita Club supported Hearts of Oak out of malice and ill will. Some degree of perspicacity is needed to be able to see the enormity of the inherent danger that this kind of unpatriotic attitude portends.

For between the lines all of us are being told that as far as some people are concerned, if only their clan's man or tribesman does not succeed to the leadership position of their country, they are even prepared to compromise the sovereignty of the nation in times of need. Some nationals are prepared to sabotage their nation when the person they would like to be president or head of state is not the one there. This is bound to be a very dangerous backwardness to be on the safest side. For if that is the case, then there is the hope that with time and education, the mentality and attitude may change for improvement. Otherwise, if this is the stuff with which the African is permanently made, then with the plurality of the societies as we have them, there can hardly be any progress, because in that case, time and education cannot effect any improvement. In Nigeria, we were told that certain vacant positions in the public services remained vacant and continue to remain vacant so long as the suitable person for the position did not come from a particular clan. There are some people who will openly proclaim that they will not drink particular brands of beer not because of their taste or quality but just because they are not brewed in their clan area. Such people distort the efforts of governments to promote the growth of local industries by urging the people to patronize goods made locally or in their own clans. Thus, like anything that can be so treated, patriotism is capable of distortions and perversions, and it is being distorted and perverted in Africa by Africans.

Perhaps Africa can learn for its own progress and development the operation and admirable attitudes to the institutions of the developed world. For example, in 1977, Mr. Ronald Reagan beat Mr. George Bush in winning the Republican Party nomination as the presidential candidate of their party. He then selected his rival Mr. Bush as his vice presidential running mate. They contested the presidential election in the United States against the Democratic Party candidates and beat them. Reagan became president and Bush became vice president of the United States of America. The significance of this was that there was no rancorous feeling against each other. Each honestly sought to be president to serve his nation to the best of each one's ability. They never denigrated each other during the campaign to win their party's nomination. Even this attitude transcends the party to which they both belonged. The two rival parties have basic agreements about their nation and differ only methodically and by degrees. Thus, where American interests are involved in anything, the leaders seek the best for the United States.

A critical examination of the British system reveals that it would be very easy to get a dictator arising in Britain, but no dictator ever arises, and the Britons know that no government of their country will ever be dictatorial. For example, Britain has a preventive detention act on its statute book, but no British government uses it to crumple on dissent, and there is mutual trust that no British government will ever use the act to stifle dissent. It would appear that respect for what is fair and just, coupled with the desire to avoid punishment of any kind, including public condemnation and resentment, strengthens the manifestation of patriotic virtues, and so it is conveniently safe to take other things for granted. Any deviation from accepted practices—what the Britons term conventions—outrages the public so much that no British government contemplates it for any moment.

It is submitted that if Awolowo and his supporters had risen above clannishness, treachery, and inordinate ethnicity and allowed Zik to be prime minister of the West for one day in 1951 when Zik's party, the NCNC, won the majority of seats in the Western Regional Assembly, Awolowo would have subsequently become, after Zik, president or prime minister of Nigeria for one million days. And today, Nigeria would have been different. This is to illustrate the extent to which goodwill and genuine patriotism could have worked for mutual benefit, which had been lost. Besides the failures displayed by the Nigerian leadership during the colonial days and the struggles against colonial rule with regard to any high sense of patriotism, the opportunity for showing truly patriotic vision first came in 1966 after the failed coup d'état. The military leaders were denied the opportunity to show their patriotic zeal by the countercoup, which distorted the process. The natural political process was first distorted by the January 1966 coup, but those who had to assume the position of leadership were denied the chance by the countercoup.

The assumption of the leadership by, at that time, Lieutenant Colonel Yakubu Gowon as head of state was accidental and a distortion of the military process. There could not have been a civil war if those who seized power at the centre in the countercoup in the middle of 1966 had shown some remorse for the killings, which were directed mainly against the Ibo people. The murder of Sir Ahmadu Bello, Sir Tafawa Balewa, and others was still more wrong all around. The failure of General Aguiyi-Ironsi's administration to execute those responsible for those murders was seen as implicit endorsement of the act and not in the light of avoidance of further bloodshed. The uprisings that resulted in the murder of General Ironsi and Colonel Fajuyi were barbaric and unfortunate. The civil war would have been averted if a more mature patriotic action had come from the centre. It is submitted that the use of military action in subduing the supposed secession was not the only solution, nor was it, in fact, the right solution. If sympathy toward those who were brutally murdered and their dependents and relations was shown from the centre, it would have split the rightly or wrongly aggrieved Nigerians in the East, and Colonel Ojukwu would not have declared the Republic of Biafra. But sober judgment failed both sides. The centre, i.e. the federal government controlled by the North, felt that the Easterners killed their leader, and they were therefore bent on wrecking their vengeance. The other side thought that the rest of Nigeria did not want them. One cannot ignore here the possible criticism by others that one is indulging in ex post facto rationalization of what happened, but the defense to that is that discussing patriotism, which, by definition, must have inclusive benefits, cannot be meaningful without any illustration with known events. And an analysis of events in Nigeria between 1966 and 1989 offers good illustration in this regard.

The bitter truth was that at that time, except for the efforts of Aguiyi-Ironsi, the Nigerian Armed Forces did not have a strong leadership with truly patriotic vision. Their underlying motivation was not to make a nation from the various heterogeneous units. The obsession was how to gain economic advantage or cripple those they suspect to have the economic power, or at least to weaken their base. Until 1966, the young up-and-coming educated lads were eager for progress, but they had political constraints. Opposed to this group were the reactionaries who felt that certain sections of the Nigerian people were becoming economically too powerful. They believed that it was necessary to reduce their economic power. These two opposing groups were broadly identifiable in the Southeastern part of the federation and the North respectively. A third group cashed in and took advantage of the ensuing hiatus to propel themselves up economically; they were the opportunists. The unhealthy aspect of it all was the apparent tendency to make political power the main economic springboard.

All this pointed to the fact that the various ethnic groups in Nigeria did not regard other ethnic groups as their own fellows. Yet this recognition that all citizens of the federation are one and the same people is the basic and only requirement for the requisite patriotic vision that can cohesively knit the people of the federation together. The recognition of all citizens of Nigeria as one people still continued to elude the federation. Certain political actions by people in authority both during and after the war tended to buttress the view that there was really no patriotic vision to make a cohesive nation, and the civil war was an ethnoeconomic war. The needed practical steps for disproving this view have not been forthcoming in official decisions on public policy.

The Oil Factor in Nigeria

The adage "Charity begins at home" has often been abused in the Nigerian context because the meaning of the word *home* has always been distorted and perverted in Nigeria. We have to begin discussing the influence of the oil factor in Nigeria, trying to resolve a riddle of a queer and abstruse dichotomy. The dichotomy is the separation of the human element in an area from the geographical or physically material features of the land. The suggestion, in other words, is that we must try to separate the human beings who occupy or belong to an area from the geographical features of the area so that we can love and enjoy the endowments of the area (whether they are kept in the area or transported by any means from that area to where we want them) and, at the same time, quite conveniently refuse or reject the human beings who come from that geographical area. This proposition may appear as abstruse to readers as the phenomenon itself. But we shall presently get to grips with its practicalities in the Nigerian context. A Nigerian must have a home as of right anywhere in the federation according to his choice and desire. The entitlement to a home anywhere in the country also gives automatically every Nigerian the right to employment anywhere in the country. The only conditions being the choice of the individual, the capability of the person, the temperamental attitudes, and the suitability of the individual for the type of job. And every Nigerian must be free to be self-employed anywhere in the federation. It naturally follows, therefore, that if a section of the people cannot be accepted in certain parts of the federation on the excuse that they do not belong there, the economic benefits available in their areas, too, should not be extended to the areas where the local policy would not accommodate those others from other parts of the country. More succinctly put, the practical point in issue is that petroleum oil found on the shores toward the eastern part of the country belongs to Nigeria, but it is a deposit found in particular areas. Patriotism cannot allow the enjoyment of the benefits of the oil by only the people in whose areas the oil deposits are situated.

So if oil pipelines are laid from Port Harcourt to Kaduna, it is unpatriotic for the Kaduna state government or anybody to deny employment to people from Port Harcourt or any other part of the country because they are not indigenes. For by denying them employment, they are automatically also denying them residence in Kaduna and the right to enjoy in Kaduna the benefits of the oil that has been pumped there. The foregoing instance is only to illustrate the point that patriotism must necessarily encompass the whole country. The retrograde idea that people from other areas are strangers who only want to come and take one's money away must necessarily be jettisoned. To stick to this notion in any guise or form is unpatriotic and should be condemned. For this kind of mentality can also go around. The wealth of petroleum oil having come from the southeastern part of the federation was taken away when it was piped to Kaduna in the north. If there is no special rule that certain people have the right to enjoy everything anywhere in the federation while others have the right to enjoy things only in their states of origin, then there should not be any form of discrimination among citizens of the federation. The valid argument is that the wealth embedded beneath the soil of any land belongs to the owner of the land. It is perverse to deny that the oil deposits in Nigeria belong to the people who live on the land or occupy the areas where the oil deposit is found. If it is tapped to other areas of the land, it is because those areas form part of Nigeria. If some people from other areas of the land should be denied the enjoyment of facilities in certain areas, then benefit from other areas should not extend to the areas where benefits are denied. The final result will be that there will be no nation. People who do not care about this or fail to advert their minds to this state of affairs are no patriots in any sense. A contrary facultative approach is to think of subjugation of the people of certain areas, which is not nation building either.

It is imperative to direct public affairs in such a way that anything deemed likely to give cause for negative thinking should be avoided. Subjugation is a negative thought. But appearances may make it inevitably occurring to people's minds. For there are strong agitations among both Nigerians and non-Nigerians alike about the calamitous civil war that ended in 1970. Some of the things on which some people expend their minds and energy may be wasteful or even wistful. For example, people query the following:

1. Whether the East would have tried to secede at all if no oil deposits were discovered there and in the Delta areas.
2. Whether the federal authorities or the North, in particular, would not have allowed the secession to hold with glee if there were no oil fields in the East.
3. Whether the significance of the abandoned properties issue does not underpin the view that it was the wealth and industry of the

Easterners and the Ibo people, in particular, that mattered to the rest of the Nigerians and not a desire to make a cohesive nation as such that urged them to fight the civil war.

4. Whether it would not have been a more patriotic act on the part of the East to have declared a more steadfast stand to fight to reinstate themselves in the normal scheme of things in Nigeria rather than try to secede after the middle 1966 pogrom. Some people even question what British attitude both official and unofficial would have been during the hostilities if no oil deposits had been found in the East and thereabouts or if the oil deposit were found elsewhere in the federation and not the eastern province.

Any attempt at trying to answer these questions by analyzing the issue would be so prospective that there is no need trying. However, the significant thing noteworthy is that certain thoughts can be provoked if public policy leans to certain directions while other thoughts occur to one's mind when a different policy is adopted. The suggestion is that the Nigerian public should be such that healthy, positive thoughts, which can promote social intercourse, must be induced for a cohesively united Nigeria to be made in which all citizens of ail groups can engage in normally healthy competition in all undertakings anywhere for excellence and drive to be rewarded and encouraged. There were three post–civil war opportunities for statesmanship and patriotic zeal and vision. The fourth opportunity was the innovative experiment under the administration of General Babangida. The Babangida experiment was a test case. One would have wished that it succeeded, but he aborted it himself. The three other previous opportunities are to be examined presently. They are as follows:

1. The responsibility of composing peace and making a nation after the civil war, which rested upon General Yakubu Gowon and his advisers

2. The decision and process of returning Nigeria to constitutional government by General Olusegun Obasanjo and his group

3. The test of democratic and smooth change of government, culminating in the elections in 1983 under Alhaji Shehu Shagari and his National Party of Nigeria

4.   The innovative experiment of the Armed Forces Ruling Council.[9]

It has been observed elsewhere that the civil war was unwarranted and that it took place at all was unfortunate. It did not end early enough, and when it ended, there should have been the fullest expression of magnanimity. However, the world did not see that. The world heard that there was no victor and no vanquished. Yet the properties of the vanquished were seized and declared abandoned. Their accounts in any bank were obliterated and made to start all over again. The vanquished were denied economic and financial opportunity of investments in a new dispensation of "indigenization." In practical terms, the vanquished were actually treated like captives of war and suppressed in any sense. There were to be no victor and no vanquished in speech but victors and vanquished in practice. The idea of abandoned property was rendered meaningless since nobody, in fact, vacated his home. It was this singular act that more than anything else gave the lie to any desire to compel all sections to reintegrate. It rather confirmed by demonstration that there was a desire to reduce or cripple the economic power of the vanquished. The reality was that the kind of vigor that normally characterizes social activities after national or international calamities was perverted and distorted in the Nigerian context. The measuring rod for determining statesmanship or patriotism was found in the extent to which a man or leader was held to have helped one or the other section of the country to succeed as against another instead of considering what was deemed as beneficial and good for the country as a whole.

The yardstick was therefore never universal. Greatness was thus to be measured in terms of the military dexterity that was displayed in waging the war and never in any magnanimous act of any leader as a statesman to benefit all sections and generations of Nigeria.

The second occasion on which patriotism and statesmanship would have been on display was the return of Nigeria to civil rule or constitutional government, which the General Obasanjo regime voluntarily decided to

---

9   Decree No. 27 of 1989 (Nigeria).

do in 1979. The exercise was marred by an apparent obsession of the then outgoing regime to hand over power to only a particular set of leadership and never to an equally particularized leadership. It was this obsession that influenced the decision to thwart the carrying out of the electoral process to the full under the 1979 Constitution, which required that there should be a second election between the best two candidates where results were indecisive. The outgoing regime of Obasanjo was afraid that one of their dreaded candidates or groups would eventually win. The government therefore descended to a rather shameful perversion and distortion in which the highest court of the land, the Supreme Court of Nigeria, ridiculed itself in aiding the government in a supposed calculation of two-thirds of nineteen states. Thus, the highly patriotic decision to return the country to constitutional government voluntarily was rather carried out in unstatesmanlike manner for reasons that can be anything but honorable. The chief justice of Nigeria later said that the decision of the Supreme Court on two-thirds of nineteen states was never to be cited in any court of the land. Apparently, it was only to please Obasanjo.

The malady was to have been righted in 1983, as another opportunity for display of statesmanship came. But it was rendered so farcical that once more, another excuse and opportunity for a military coup d'état was found, which wrestled the government again sadly from the civilians. In all these circumstances, patriotism and statesmanship were thrown away by the leadership involved.

The challenges thrown by the Babangida innovations were viewed by many in the light of the past experiences enumerated above. There was a "voluntary" decision to return the country to constitutional government in 1992. Some political measures, quite controversial, were taken to prevent the nasty elements of ethnicity and religion from marring the smooth transition. At the top of the priorities of those in authority was how to prevent ethnic or any form of other parochial consideration from disturbing the politico-social arrangements in the country. This factor persuaded the government in its decision to issue first an executive flat and later the transition to civil rule (political parties regulation and activities) decree, making it a legal rule that "there shall be only two political parties in the federation, namely, [a] the National Republican Convention and [b] the Social Democratic Party."

The two parties were formed and named by the government for the people. Each Nigerian citizen was expected to join one of the two parties at his own free will. He, after joining, could seek an elected office in the party. However, innovations were found in the facts that not only were the parties formed by the government for the people to join but the manifestos of the two parties were also drawn by the government for the prospective party members and officials. By S3 and Schedule 1 of the decree, the government formulated guiding principles in the form of ideals and precepts for those who would seek the people's mandate for leadership. For example, it was provided that the composition of the government of the federation, the conduct of public affairs, and the operation of any of the agencies of the government must be carried out to reflect the federal character of Nigeria and the need to promote national unity. It was also required that government policy must be carried out to reflect the federal character of Nigeria and the need to promote national unity. It was also required that government must be such that national loyalty must be fostered by the state among the citizens.

One of the most interesting provisions in Schedule 1 of the decree was the provision that the state should encourage intermarriage among persons from different places of origin or people belonging to different religions and ethnic groups and also encourage associations that cut across ethnic differences etc. These ideals were mostly desirable and obvious enough. But who was to provide the leadership or the framework for these ideals to be met? The decree was saying that real patriotism must animate the acts and conduct of people who sought leadership positions in the country. And this, in fact, was to state the obvious. The politics of Africa and of Nigeria, more than any other country, had always centered on these ideals. It was how to conduct the affairs of the state in order to achieve those ideals, which must and needed to be spelled out. There was the need for innovative sanctions to be provided for acts and public conduct that should derogate from realizing those ideals. There was the need for the government to cut the path for the people with cutlass. The political leadership was to provide the hoes and shovels and spades for the people to make the smooth road or path to the prosperous land envisaged.

The clear suggestion here is that there should be legislations not necessarily criminal but necessarily enforceable that should abolish all forms of discrimination in employment anywhere in the federation. Then ail the provisions in the decree would have been taken care of automatically without those express provisions. So long as there is a feeling that some states are educationally disadvantaged, those states will always be looked upon as such without improvement. Other states will also strive to get so qualified. Supposed it is discovered or established that some states are also economically or financially disadvantaged, can there be discriminatory policies in favour of such states or communities? A man in his right senses cannot think of getting married when he is unemployed. The young Fulani lady will not be attracted to the young Yoruba man who is denied employment in Sokoto state on account of "non-indigene." And so be it quite similarly in other states and ethnic groups. But when the government enacts that the word *indigene* should not be the criterion for anything in the federation, then the fears that animated the enactment that federal character must be reflected in public policy is taken care of.

The position was made worse by the fact that the manifestos of the two legal parties were drawn by the government for the parties. In fact, it was the General Babangida regime that formed parties and invited people to come and join them. The constitutions of the parties were drawn by the creator of the parties, and their manifestos were formulated by the government for prospective leaders to implement after joining the parties. None of the two parties actually included in its manifesto how clearly it proposed to promote social integration in Nigeria. The reality, however, is that the feeling of belonging and loyalty cannot be imposed; it is always a realization within the individual. And in spite of all the slogans on the radio or on the screens of television sets, if Nigeria should continue to emphasize federal character in constitutional arrangements and the states continue to stress the idea of "indigene" and stick to it, then internally the sense of belonging will always be divided.

Loyalty and the sense of belonging may, however, probably go to Nigeria when a citizen is out of the country. This cannot be a healthy phenomenon, but it will be dictated as a natural consequence of internal conduct of public affairs. The result will be that there will be several nations internally while one Nigeria will be falsely portrayed to the outside world. The solution to this is clearly an issue for the leadership at the centre. The problem can be more conveniently tackled and solved by a divine intervention since the solution will necessarily constitute a revolution in the people's way of thinking, and revolution can always be better handled by extra constitutional measures and government.

Conclusion

Patriotism, nationalism, and statesmanship are animated by the same qualities that encompass the overall goodness of the society to which one belongs. The required quality is therefore based on inclusive benefit and not altruism. There are difficulties involved in all human activities, but the needed quality is demonstrable at all levels. The African context is made more complex because of the heterogeneity of the societies and the continuity of nation building. Africa's patriotic vision requires that one must see beyond ethnic and religious groups, and those leaders of Africa who capitalized on religion and ethnicity to propel themselves into the leadership of parochial sections were no statesmen or patriots since such people necessarily conducted their affairs in utter derogation of mutual trust, respect, and goodwill. The Nigerian Civil War presents different facets and several dichotomies. If Nigeria can use the calamitous experience to its advantage to grow stronger and united, the vestiges of the civil war ought to have been obliterated as soon as the war was over, but this has not been possible because the civil war was not waged purely as a patriotic war. It was ethnic in the sense of attempting to annihilate an ethnic group and economic in the sense that there was a desire that the wealth associated with that ethnic group be assimilated. The government at the centre had a duty to correct the bad impression the state of affairs has created because of the oil factor.

So long as the dichotomies persist, negative thought will occur to people's minds, and their sense of belonging and loyalty will be dampened. It is in this light that the abuse of the post–civil war opportunities remains regrettable. Innovations of the Babangida administration were very challenging, but they seemed to have left out the practical issues and rather reiterated the obvious ideals in the provisions of the enactments seeking to remove the sociopolitical bottleneck from the federation. The fundamental issue centers on the continued stress being put on federal character. For this, in turn, fails to compel the states to de-emphasize ethnicity.

However, if the various states continue to stick fast to their sensitivity to the employment opportunity to the youths and refuse to ignore the ethnic or "indigene" syndrome, the Nigerian national unity will continue to suffer. And in that case, only a divine intervention can provide the solution *to revolutionize the thought processes of the people.*

The Element of Aburi Influence in Attempting to Avoid the Civil War

After the 1966 pogrom, the federal government represented by the North and the Easterners were unable to draw close to each other for any dialogue. The military government of Ghana, led by General J. A. Ankrah, decided to act toward preventing any military confrontation. The military leadership of Ghana organized a meeting of the Nigerian military leaders at Aburi in Ghana to try to iron out their differences. The Nigerian leaders did not bring their attorneys general to Aburi. Only the soldiers were there. The Ghanaian counterparts served as mediators to give assurance of safety. In a nutshell, the decision arrived at in Aburi was that the two factions suspecting each other be allowed to stay slightly apart for cool air to blow.

But Britain and British influence must be to blame in shouting out their suspicion that Nigeria would break up. Britain did not want to see a break up of Nigeria, yet Britain would not like to see any compromise that would produce, in British view, a situation that would bring the Southern and Northern Nigeria on equal footing in the government. So this attitude influenced the rest of the Nigerians not to accept anything or arrangement favorable to the East apparently. So going back home to Nigeria, the influence and advice of the West, which was Yoruba, heavily under the guidance of Britain through Taslim Elias, then federal attorney general, and Obaferni Awolowo and Co, who were die-hard Yoruba bigots, decided that they should use military force rather than any temporary arrangement made at Aburi, Ghana, to cushion tempers for cool air to blow, and civil war broke out in result with suspect British neutrality.

It is ever regrettable that in the 1950s, Britain and its Nigerian allies rejected Dr. Nnamdi Azikiwe's enlightened proposal that Nigeria be divided into many semiautonomous states based on geographical rather than ethnic factors with a strong centre. The British press called Zik's proposal "six-foot stupidity" and castigated Zik as wanting Britain to create for him an empire to supervise. Today the Nigerians have found it fit to implement that Zikist idea by creating a strong centre and a new federal capital at Abuja in the heart of the federation. This enlightenment needs to go around, and a Nigerian must be accorded all the civic rights and responsibility based on his or her domicile and not "indigene." The absence of this seems to be the bane hitching up Nigeria's development as a cohesively strong federation.

CHAPTER FIVE

EDUCATION FOR ERADICATION OF ILLITERACY, IGNORANCE, AND POVERTY

A lot has been said about the free senior high school concept in Ghana, but there should be no pretension that it has been exhaustive.

The concept of education is quite wide in scope, and the importance of education is not of any peculiar emphasis to any country but a universal necessity to all mankind. No nation can afford to neglect the education of its citizens is not a cliché. However, when education is emphasized in Ghana or Africa, it is because the problems of Africa are such that every solution to them must be commensurate with their intensity, enormity, and complexity. Ignorance and illiteracy are the phenomena that readily come to mind when one thinks of education because they are the phenomena against which educational efforts are directly supposed to be addressed. It will be absolutely wrong, however, to assert that ignorance and illiteracy alone are the ills that education should seek to eradicate. The elimination of the incidence of disease and squalidness, making it possible for further understanding of the world, and the enhancement of economic conditions of the educated individuals cumulate to enhance the conditions of the nation-state. Yet several factors go into making these possible, and education is the most significant one.

The Meaning of Education

The special thing about education is that the mere mention of it seems to be enough definition of it. Everybody seems to have some idea as to what education means because it has to do with the bringing up and training of a person. It is formal when it involves a systematic training and instruction given to persons in schools or colleges. The composite results of such systematic training and instruction are also referred to as education. It is informal when the composite results are achieved without any formally systematic training and instruction necessarily arranged by any external agent other than the individual himself. It can therefore be said that education consists of the knowledge, skills and abilities, and character acquisition and development that manifest themselves from a formal or informal process of deliberately instructional training and direction in any process by which a person is enabled to acquire and develop those qualities.

Differences can be found not only in education being formal or informal. There are also various types of education. There is purely academic endeavour that lays emphasis on academic performance, which, in most cases, is determined in a formal examination. There is that type of education that emphasizes the training of the individual to acquire a skill in a profession or trade, which sometimes combines the academic measure with it. There is still yet the informal education that may not be formally tested by way of organized examinations of any type to prove or ascertain the attainment of any prescribed standard but that may manifest itself practically as the individual interacts with others in society. Incidentally, this type of education cannot obtain many professions; the basic formal education must necessarily be first acquired. In any case, it would appear that at one stage or the other, a certain degree of formality is needed basically. However, about a general education that comprises the acquisition of knowledge and its development—the development of a propitious individual character—perhaps more can be said in favour of informal education that continues, and it may be considered as the best type of general education and probably the rarest too.

Every society needs all the various forms of education, because skilled manpower is needed as well as excellence in all endeavors. Our aims in education should be the production of articulate and understanding citizenry who are sagacious in counseling solutions and, above all, who are of propitious character and responsible and devoid of all forms of petty spite and mischief. We must produce citizenry by whom virtues will be not only recognized and acknowledged but also appreciated and admired, citizenry that will constantly strive to do right and avoid mischief not necessarily for the purpose of avoiding punishment but more so because it is right and just. Thus, an educated person is expected to act and behave in certain ways in certain circumstances.

Society ascribes certain attributes to a person who is educated. Certain persons, because of their professional calling, necessarily need certain types of education, sometimes specialized and/or additional to the type of education that is supposed to propitiously affect the general character of the citizenry. All persons require the general type, but not all persons require the specialized type of education. The problem in education does not seem to lie in the provision of specialized education for technical and professional skills acquisition and development. This is not saying there is sufficiency in that direction and no problem at all. It is that because there are ready means of testing and recording satisfaction in this kind of educational programme, the problems there are not abstruse and subtle as such. The same cannot be readily stated in the direction of the general type of education, which every person in the society needs without exception, because education is not achieving desirable results in this direction.

It is sadder still to note that disappointing trends are even more rampant in leadership positions in institutions of higher learning in spite of commendable efforts by educationists and governments thinking about their work and drawing programmes for implementing research results, and yet the character of the individual citizen is not propitiously affected at all by the results of educational programmes. People exhibit various kinds of mentality or mindset that make the conscious person who interacts with them to entertain rather forlorn hopes. It is worse still when one comes to meet experiences in employment at workplaces. Some people behave toward their fellows as if they had no heart or conscience. There is sadism displayed by some in authority wantonly for the sake of it. Others are engaged in organized and concerted effort to destroy their fellows for the sake of doing so. Organized PHD (pull him down) meetings plan mischief to "pull others down." "He is too arrogant," "He is too big in his shoes," "He is trying to know too much" are common statements simply because someone wants to look at things dispassionately and from a more detached position than before, and they will really pull him down.

So education is not favorably affecting the citizenry. Education is not having any propitious effect on the character of the citizenry. Education is not improving the mental process of people. It is a matter of greater concern when it is realized that this inexplicable trend, which can justifiably be found with the stark illiterate, is displayed in a more outrageous form by some university dons who pervert logic in arguments to justify mischief. Thus, articulation of the intellect, which is aided by education, is misdirected by the scholar, and the stark illiterate observing this trend easily becomes bewildered. Otherwise, a previous or current act of one highly educated person—professor or lecturer or any other lettered entity—can easily be cited by a nonscholar to everyone's embarrassment.

Many people advance many different reasons for this state of affairs. One explanation is that education is generally exotic, and as such, different persons absorb it and react to it differently. Some are really good, but in every situation, good things are rare and uncommon. Therefore, there are still other highly placed scholars who may have favorable influences, but they are rather more reserved. Another school of thought argues that poverty has eaten so deep into the system that its influence, which is grossly adverse, has negative effect on the way educational absorption manifests itself. It is not that education has no effect on the character of the citizenry but that the conditions for mischief drive are such that it appears odd to do otherwise. Ethnic and tribal elements aggravate the situation. This, coupled with religious differences, the rate of absorption in education, and how people react to what they have absorbed, is thus affected rather negatively. It is argued that all the foregoing factors would not have been problems in normal circumstances but for the fact that man is a complex entity.

The Impact of Education

An attempt has been made to demonstrate that education has not been doing what it ought to be doing, but the explanation offered for this tendency ended on a note of vicious cycle whose pivot, the human being must be educated. The implied assertion is that man is essentially a limited person. Since education is exotic to many, the favorable attitude to adopt is to view the effect or impression of education as an impact of ideas on limited people. It is intended to proceed now from here because one cannot see the solution to the problem anywhere other than in education.

It is education that can create propensities that will make the behaviours of the general citizenry always socially approbatory. This atmosphere is necessary for any comprehensive social progress in harmony or with little friction. For this to be achieved, the word *education* must be taken in its compendious term to be meaningful (the development of the person all around). It is concerned with the making of a man or woman.

Education must make every man know and appreciate what is fair and just in any context. But it should not end there. Man must also be made to try and attain always that which is fair and just. Man must be able to decide at the appropriate time and on the right occasion that a thing is just bad or not good enough and then avoid it. Education must inculcate the habit of honesty in man so that there can be trusts, and there should be the absence of treachery and suspicion so that there can be success in business and other economic transactions and relationships with reasonable mutuality. Education must teach gentleness, gratitude, neatness and cleanliness, moderation and sincerity, reasonableness and sympathy, and thoroughness in all endeavors, in addition to the acquisition and development of professional and technical skills, so that man can support himself economically and financially. Having assigned all these duties to education, it is now left for us to design the content of the courses where the courses should be held and their durations.

Forms and Content of Education

Human nature and the incidence of living would require that education must necessarily be both formal and informal. Different people go through different experiences and in diverging circumstances, so even if education is made free at all stages, it is not every person who will be able to benefit from formal education. People who are compelled to educate themselves privately are therefore limited to certain areas of study because there are many areas in which one cannot study without the help of an instructor formally so called. This condition prevents a lot of people from being educated because without formal opportunity, there is no other avenue opening for them to learn anything that is not part of the trade they have to follow for their living.

However, general education is of various stages. The first impression starts from individual homes. This is also largely informal. The informality has some effect quite subtle to describe. It is that there is often unconsciousness involved. The parents up to whom the youth looks for guidance and guardianship are often not conscious in educating the youth at home. But the youth, too, is not consciously told that he is learning anything from his parents. Everything is by impression, and it is not all impressions that are favorable for educational purposes. Thus, a snag already begins from the home. All the impressions the youth gets from very early stages at home differ from home to home. The effect, whether favorable or adverse, is often a matter of degree depending on the enlightenment or otherwise available in each home. While this may be so in every society, it is more remarkable in some societies because of the central problem about inequalities in life.

To educate implies to give intellectual and moral training. Now because the early stages of education are necessarily informal and also because education essentially begins at individual homes, it is subjective. The quality is a function of the nature of home and the environment into which the child is born. If the environment or home is good, the child starts with good advantage. If the home or environment is poor, so much the worse for the child. Good home and good environment imply educated parents and adults with whom the child or youth is likely to come in constant contact. If the greatest informal impression on the youth happens to be that "life is a wicked thing and yet we love it," his future formal education will all be centered around this concept. If the person, during his or her youthful transformation, got the impression that "the world is a savage place," this is going to permanently affect his or her attitude to life.

If in the course of further education there happens to have occurred another notion quite different, the chances will be that the new notion will be treated as an exception and not the rule. Others behaving differently may even be regarded as fools or abnormal. In fact, it would appear that this is what actually happens in actual life. A person's environmental conditions actually affect his or her facultative inclinations. Two different persons do not always see the same thing in the same light. However, education, to be desirably effective, is not to be directed toward achieving absolute uniformity in anything, nor can this be ever so. Education must make it possible for human faculties to sharpen, articulate, and not be blunted or rendered narrow and shallow. The faculties of the youth must be made to receive and accommodate, analyze and sieve ideas and phenomena with open mind. Thus, where sections of a people are subjected to perennial penury, their attitudes and their faculties and habits become conditioned by penuriousness. There is a natural tendency in such people to develop unfavorable feeling toward wealth and opulence and hate those who control or possess wealth just because they are opulent. The only reason is that there is an apprehension in the section, i.e., condemnation to perpetual squalidness. Therefore, whenever the two sections happen to be in contact with each other, there is this uneasy feeling of mutual dislike, one always suspecting the other.

It has been argued that education is what can prevent this kind of situation, and where the situation already exists, it can be removed by education. But education cannot do this without the infrastructure favorable for it. This infrastructure cannot in any way be provided by anybody other than the government. The suggestion is that a progressive and enlightened government must abandon all prestigious and grandiose projects in cities and urban centers and devote funds that would have been spent on such projects to provide good road networks all over the country, provide good drinking water to every corner of the country, provide electricity to every area of the country, and see to it that the kind of facilities and amenities meant for all in the country must be equally provided for the ordinary citizens everywhere. The government can thereafter leave the rest of their own social and material development conveniently to the people themselves. The next important matters to tackle naturally will be strategic siting of educational and health institutions in all areas to avoid the need for the common people to travel long distances before getting to schools and hospitals. Thus, in the end, the success of educational efforts cannot be isolated. It is essentially dependent upon the spread of infrastructural amenities.

The importance of all this can be seen in the fact that education progresses by stages. The formal educational ladder begins from the very elementary school through secondary school to the university. Others branch to vocational and technical school. Still, others go to polytechnic to follow various professions and trades. The skills and training that these people acquire are no ends in themselves. The provision of the needed infrastructure quite well spread will not only support the less burdensome acquisition of the skills but also create avenues for their use. The point is that these arrangements will reasonably minimize economic killings with violence etc.

The most notorious form of such killings all around is armed robbery or robbery with violence. The majority of the people involved in this most dreaded act are school leavers. School leavers, in this context, embrace all the people who have, for any reasons, left formal educational institutions. They include universities, colleges, and secondary schools, as well as polytechnics. Because the young lads leave schools and have no jobs, they become desperate. They see wealth being displayed redundantly both by public office holders in the name of the public and by private individuals. They see people living in and displaying redundant opulence while their own conditions represent the most despicable form of squalidness. Conditions have not been created to favour the idea of staying behind in their localities to enjoy, at least, the kind of things they have become used to when at school in the campuses.

Meanwhile, the values of the society generally have become perverted so that respect is accorded to wealth and wealth alone. It is even absolutely irrelevant how one acquired the wealth being displayed. In the circumstances, virtuous conduct ceases to be relevant. In employment in the public service, since virtues are irrelevant, abuses take precedence. The female counterparts who cannot secure employment resort to prostitution of various kinds, and their patronage is assured by the affluent members of the society partly because of lust and partly for the sake of being perverse. And sexual laxity, as a form of corruption, knows no bounds. So that owing to the poor infrastructure in the system, the form of education available produces an impact that rather makes it unconsciously possible for certain undesirable tendencies to manifest themselves.

The Cost of Education

Generally, the cost of education will involve all the expenses that go into the provision of education to a people. The computation will include all the tangible factors such as the provision of the overall infrastructure, like school and college buildings of all kinds; libraries and other equipment in laboratories and demonstrating workshops; teachers, lecturers, and other staff for research, maintenance, and safekeeping of equipment, research materials, and books; and also clerical and other staff. The cost of education cannot always be equally so tangible when one thinks of education that is had by individuals by their own private efforts. Many times, when people talk of the cost of education, it is in the public sector, and the first things to mention are salaries of teachers and lecturers etc. All other costs are taken for granted. Thus, when people talk of "free education," they actually mean the pupil attending classes, lectures, seminars, etc. without paying anything in the form of fees for gaining such facilities and benefits. There can be free education in only a second sense. Thus, if educational institutions provided in the public sector out of public funds are meant, then no one should talk of "free education." By whatever arrangement that can be made, education can never be free. So it is misleading to talk of "free education" as if nobody actually paid for it. Free education can be meaningful only in another sense that every person or organization must be free to set up educational institutions. Then in that sense alone, education is already free. But those who benefit from educational facilities must pay for it. Even if pupils and students do not pay anything at all for their class tutorials, board and lodging, and lectures, education is always paid for and never free. Perhaps if there is the need to be very pedantic, we may rather try to find out who pays for education and what proportion is paid. But the real challenge is to be found in how to successfully arrange things so that education will be available for everybody universally.

There have been days when a school of the desirable standard cannot be accessible unless one traveled more than one hundred miles away, i.e., to another town. This situation has not changed. In such a situation, the cost of education to the boy or girl who had to make that journey before reaching a school or college was already substantial. But the one in whose town the school or college is built did not have to meet that cost if both chaps arrived at the campus, and they did not pay anything for their tuition and boarding and lodging. It would be unintelligible to say education was free because the students paid nothing. For education to be called meaningfully free, the government must make sure that out of public funds, the infrastructural educational facilities in every town or village are the same. The staffing of every school must be equal. Every person interested will then be required to start with these provisions with equal physical efforts. This is the only sense in which any talk of "free education" can be equitably accepted. Thus, leaderships must talk of universal and not "free education."

Now it may be necessary to inquire whether it is desirable that education must be free in the proper sense as suggested here. Then it may be further asked, What kind of education is it that should be free? These issues require answers devoid of any emotions because education itself has some problems as it is now known and understood generally. These problems do not have to be found in how to provide education only but also in what education is found to be doing. Perhaps it may be said that for education to be free, its content must be revised or reexamined or even overhauled.

However, if education is made equitably free in every town and village, will there be funds and resources available for any development project in other areas? The answer is no! The content of education, as at present, tends to produce negative effect on the citizenry. Many an educated person largely tends to shy away from using his or her hand. There is general aversion to any form of physical exertion as if it were rather shameful to do so. The educational institutions provided and supported with public funds emphasize the training of the individual to be academically sound. Then elsewhere, religion is added. So a lot of people claim to be educated, but they cannot carry out simple routine examination of even the motor car they drive.

Education has been teaching people to develop foreign tastes in many respects. Added to this is what used to be emphasized language, problem, textbooks, medium of instruction, etc. Even the sciences were emphasized in their purely theoretical aspects to the detriment of any practical significance. If this state of affairs remains unoverhauled and education is made free to all in the equitable sense, the results is going to be that the population will have all the recitals being rendered to boredom while and when simple tools would break down and need servicing. So for policy and strategic reasons, it will not be desirable or advisable to make education free at all levels. It should be deemed necessary that the beneficiary of education must bear part of its costs. This will create room for equally intelligent persons to be available for all other manpower requirements. For if formal education as we know it is made absolutely free at all levels, there will be complexity of problems. Let people stop talking and thinking of "free education" because education can never be free.

It is true that the situation may create room for abuses like in all situations. Take the end of the 1950s and the middle of or the early 1960s for example. No person could gain admission to the university in Ghana without passing an examination in a general paper at the end of the secondary school sixth form course. But after 1960, President Nkrumah's government abolished the general paper, and people were admitted to the university without it. It was reintroduced after the 1966 General E. K. Kotoka military coup and made compulsory. However, when this decision was taken, the University of Ghana made a secret of it by intentionally communicating the change of decision to only certain colleges and hid the decision from the public at large. At that time, it was decided that middle-level manpower was needed, and so those who had left school and decided to work should be compelled to become satisfied with where they were. The method they used was the failure to write the general paper examination that they induced. The result was that many prospective university students who decided to work for a year or two before continuing their education in the university were denied admission because they did not write the general paper examinations. So the university authorities at the time unfairly abused the policy and thereby succeeded in preventing in fact, frustrating many young aspirants from getting university education. They denied the people the opportunity of taking part in fair competitions for admission to university.

One may wonder as to whose interest they then decided to serve other than their own and their relations and friends who were secretly informed in privacy about the university's new policy decision. That was yet another exhibition of the mindset educational problem. African leaderships must stop talking about free education because education cannot be free, and it is not even desirable that it should be free absolutely since that will leave no funds for development efforts in other directions. Another point of interest is that even if education is really made free equitably, a lot of people, for various reasons, cannot benefit from it because education really goes beyond merely being able to read and write. This is clearly manifested in the common experience of all, except that it can be wantonly denied that a lot of African elderly men and women display a great deal of wisdom and seasoned intelligence in speech and actions and conduct in their everyday affairs and experiences even though they did not lay any claim to any formal education. It will be wasteful trying to speculate what would have been their lot if these people had been formally educated.

At the same time, there are so many university-degree holders and even senior members of university institutions whose mental horizons are retrograde, parochial, and even destructive. It will be equally wasteful trying to imagine what such people would have been if they had not been formally educated when they display the kind of mentality they have in spite of being highly educated. For education to be satisfactory, it must be universal. It does not have to be free to be universal. Education needs to be qualitative too and not perfunctory to be successful. This can be achieved by directing more equitably the distribution of the nation's wealth and income. Free education is an unintelligible phrase that has become a slogan for seeking popularity based on treachery and ignorance.

CHAPTER SIX

GHANA—THE FACTORS THAT FACILITATED THE SUCCESS OF TYRANNICAL DICTATORSHIP (1958–1966)

British Gold Coast Sophistés

The British colonial administrators were not bothered about ethnicity, so they created Trans-Volta District of the colony, making Akusey its headquarters. That district stretched from Ada to Senchi through Keta, Anyako to Aflao through Denu, Agotime Kpetoe to Bame, Kpeve, Tsibu, Todome, Tsate, Kpatime, Boso Anum, Toseng, Onayo, Peki, Akwamu, Kome/Kpong, etc., comprising Ewes, Guangs, Ga Adangbes, etc.

There was at one time in those days Peki-Guang Local Council prior to the plebiscite of 1956. While the colonial authorities concerned themselves with geographical factors, the first nationalist government of Nkrumah should have done better to avoid using ethnicity as the basis for creating districts and regions. Ghana is a heterogeneous unitary republic.

After the 1956 plebiscite, the Volta Region should have been created solely on geographical basis to cover areas inhabited by Guangs, Ashantis (which Nkunya and Worawora people claim to be), Ewes, Kyerepongs, Bueman,

Adeles, etc. to form a replica of the Ghanaian nation concentrating in one region to have made it impossible for any person or party to rely on ethnicity to win elections there. This would have been one of the prides of Africa. On the contrary, the administration of Akufo-Addo tended to be disappointingly hell-bent on stratifying the country further on ethnic lines. Their aim seems to be to avoid a republic and any replica. Their idea seems to be to desire to follow Busia in using the word *Akan* to suppose that by that word or name, the rest of Ghanaians who are not Akan will become or be treated as peripheries. People of this group did not seem to believe in anything other than creating dynastic hegemony. They are opposed to republicanism.

Kwame Nkrumah had every opportunity on earth to be a great man, but he abused it. Instead of leading a united Ghana, Nkrumah chose to enact a preventive detention law, which he used in his ambition to become an emperor of any possible area of Africa, using Ghana as a springboard. Certainly, a proper leadership and enlightened mindset will emerge and make Republican Ghana grow strong and stable. Any shadow of a dynastic hegemony will become only a passing temporary fizzle, which will fizzle out soon, and the triumph of the stable Republic of Ghana will be realized.

Political Trends in the Country on the Eve of Independence

The opponents of Nkrumah feared his communist and totalitarian proclivity, but the masses did not know or understand communism or socialism, and those who saw the communist trend had to support the CPP as the better of two evils—the other evil being colonial subjugation. The conscious political opponents of Nkrumah and his CPP found it too difficult to educate the masses to understand the "isms" with which they were being inundated. Consequentially, the masses were left to remain obsessed with the promise of the CPP that the white man will leave the country and Ghanaians would become their own masters.

In the preface to his *Autobiography of Kwame Nkrumah*, immediately after Ghana's independence in 1957, Nkrumah wrote: "At this time I devoted much energy to the study of revolutionaries and their methods. Those who interested me most were Hannibal, Cromwell, Napoleon, Lenin, Mazzini, Gandhi, Mussolini and Hitler." After breaking away from the United Gold Coast Convention (UGCC) and forming the Convention People's Party (CPP), Nkrumah's charisma and popularity soared, and he had the support of able men like K. A. Gbedemah, C. T. Nylander, N. A. Welbeck, Archie Casely-Hayford, E. Ako-Adjei, Kojo Botsio, E. O. Asafu Ajaye, J. H. Allasani, Imoru Egala, Mumuni Bawumia, etc., most of whom broke away from the UGCC to propel Nkrumah to snatch the leadership of the independence struggle from J. B. Danquah and the UGCC. These and many more others were the actual founders who nurtured the Ghanaian nation. Nkrumah alone could never have done that. A British Communist Party membership card was found on Nkrumah when he was arrested, but he publicly denied that he was a communist. While his closest supporters and lieutenants had no doubt about his communist inclinations, they daftly supposed that because communism cannot gain any root in Ghana, Nkrumah could not succeed as a tyrant. They believed that the nature of the Ghanaian would not accommodate communism. But right from the very beginning, there were clear indicators as to what Nkrumah would later become. Thus, the failure in the direction to recognize and acknowledge the worthy contributions of others in making the Ghanaian nation led to the fall of the first republic, because unbridled sycophancy cannot make a healthy society. It has to be conceded that if these separatist groups had succeeded in their desires and methods as against the CPP, I suspect that there would have been probably no Ghana as we have it today.

As far as the masses were concerned, political events in the country from 1949 to 1957 were centered on the Convention People's Party, which was perceived as the vanguard of the agitation for freedom from colonial rule, such that all other groups were deemed as in opposition to Nkrumah and the CPP. There, however, existed a keen competition between the CPP and the numerous other political groupings for the leadership of the independence struggle and the power to rule. As the case may be, the voice of this myriad of other groupings was muted and overshadowed by the more strident and mass appeal propaganda onslaught of the CPP, and so the masses failed to recognize and identify the other groupings as part of the fighting force against colonial domination. This turn of events can be credited more to the method than just the content of the propaganda drive of the CPP.

In method, extreme populism was one strategy employed, at the centre of which Kwame Nkrumah was cast as a demigod and deified. This method was effective in achieving its purpose of popularizing Nkrumah as the only one capable of wresting power from the colonialists for Africans.

Another strategy was to draw the masses of the people into believing that their aspirations for nationhood and self-realization was tied to the independence struggle and that these issues cannot wait till a later time; else, the opportunity would be lost forever. Although there was an element of truth in these methodological precepts, much of it had to do with whipping up those sentiments that lie at the very core of the expectations of the people and simultaneously telling the people in reverse that they by themselves cannot achieve them, except by the party for the people. In effect, the propaganda method of the CPP eventually succeeded in making the party a mass People's Party, but one which did not truly belong to the people but personified and embodied the singularity of Nkrumah as the central icon. R. S. Iddrisu was the CPP candidate in 1956 for elections to the National Assembly, representing Tamale Central Constituency. After an avalanche of propagandist oration and the wild applause following the formal introduction of the candidate by Ako-Adjei, Nkrumah casually took over the microphone and said jocularly, "Don't mind him. Look at me. He is representing me."

Comical as this would seem, it was an early warning sign of the personality characteristics of a tyrant-in-the-making, but who would see it in the heat of the times and to resist it or raise the alarm bells? In effect, the masses of the people can then be said to have actively contributed to the self-centricism and eventual tyrannical manifestations demonstrated by Kwame Nkrumah in the political life of the nation. In the opening lines of his Midnight Speech to herald the dawn of independence at the Old Polo Grounds in Accra, Nkrumah said, "Yes, I made everything clear . . ." This statement is never a trivial one. It is pregnant with second meaning. Nkrumah was all. Everything and everyone else was insignificant—a truly totalitarian trait. But again, this was not immediately discerned, nor was there enough concentrated opposing power to combat or negate it. The CPP had no elected officers. There was no chairman, there was no treasurer, there was no secretary, etc. Tyrannical dictatorship started from the CPP leadership.

As it were, the CPP managed to seize the limelight and leadership of the independence struggle not only by manipulation of the minds of the ordinary masses but also through a conscious implementation of certain political tactics embedded in well-thought-out organizational strategy, which itself was essentially driven by propaganda. The "saturation strategy," which called for the consistent delivery of a particular message repetitively, was employed to simultaneously drive home firstly the message of what was required, secondly to create a particular worldview and mindset in the masses, and thirdly to elicit a particular spontaneous reaction by which to achieve an ultimate objective. Throughout the electioneering campaign in 1956, the message of the CPP remained the same in the North, the Colony (as the Southern Province was called), in Ashanti (which did not exclude Brong-Ahafo), and in the Togoland (the present Volta and Oti Regions). The message re-echoed: "Our plan and aim is to put together the Colony and Ashanti, Togoland and the Northern Territories, and then we manage our own affairs." Surely, this message would sound sensible, plausible, and persuasive to the masses. In fact, this was the main strategy and purpose strongly uniting the UGCC under J. B. Danquah's leadership, which was snatched by the CPP leaders, breaking away from the UGCC in 1948, and it catapulted Nkrumah into the political leadership of the Gold Cost (Ghana).

Opposed to this were the separatist groups whose champions were Busia and Dombo. S. G. Antor and Ayeke group of the Togo Congress Party (TCP) was mainly opposed to Nkrumah's leadership of the CPP as many activities of Nkrumah from the onset proved to be tyrannically dictatorial. Nkrumah cleverly and systematically thwarted any election of party officers. He persistently claimed that there was a need to present a united front, as if electing a party chairman, party treasurer, party secretary, etc. would make the CPP not united. This made many other politically influential personalities who also broke away from the UGCC—such as Victor Owusu, Joe Appiah, Dr. Kurankyi Taylor, R. R. Amponsah, and many others—to refuse to have anything to do with the CPP. The result was that Busia advocated a federation, and Dombo leadership in the North preached that the heterogeneous ethnic entities in the North should ignore their diverging ethnicity and make a state of their own, after which they would decide on how to relate with the South.

The people of the North rejected this idea and voted for the CPP. The heterogeneous unitary state of Ghana then came into being. So the impact of that UGCC campaign message snatched by the CPP achieved a dual objective. First of all, the overwhelming masses of the people rallied around the red, white, and green flag of the CPP, thereby strengthening and stamping Nkrumah's authority and leadership on the independence movement. Secondly, and more importantly, it also made the political work of all those opposed to Nkrumah's leadership, as well as the task of opponents of the CPP, to win the hearts and minds of the electorate a very difficult task. Rather than study the situation objectively and taking calculated countermeasures, the other groups in opposition resorted to certain actions and methods that made things more difficult for them politically. They made the masses of the people not to see them as a part of the fighting force to break the colonial yoke.

Meanwhile, it is significant to note that the United Gold Coast Convention (UGCC), the first organized anticolonial forum of indigenous Africans from which Kwame Nkrumah and others broke away to form the CPP, had fizzled out of any serious political contention by 1949, remaining in oblivion since then. To fill this important vacuum and in response to the urgent need to create a kind of opposition to the CPP, a number of political groups emerged and formally launched themselves onto the preindependence political arena. They were as follows: Ghana Congress Party (GCP), formed and led by Dr. Kofi Abrefa Busia; Anlo Youth Organization (AYO), whose secretary was M. K. Apaloo; Muslim Youth Association (MYA); Togo Congress Party (TCP); Northern People's Party (NPP); and National Liberation Movement. In addition to these seven official groups, there was a local tribal group, or more specifically, an uprising in Accra, i.e., the *Ga Shifimo Kpee*, a limited and purely tribal movement that did not amount to any serious or significant political presence beyond traditional Accra and was stillborn. Its slogan was "Gbon gbe wo" (Strangers are killing us). With the political consciousness of the people being preconditioned as it were by the propaganda of the CPP, the electorate perceived all these groups as opponents to the CPP who were bent on violence to destroy the forward march of the CPP toward independence, which was eventually achieved on March 6, 1957.

Another mistake of the other political groups was to preach federalism and separation of a sort in counterpoint to the call by the CPP to weld the territories that would constitute the new Ghana into a single unitary whole. In that state of affairs, and owing to the massive support it had gathered from the masses, the Convention People's Party, which had now clearly won the leadership of the independence movement, systematically became a monstrous organization monopolized by Nkrumah. The other groupings failed to unite into a cohesive opposing force until after independence. But the balance of political forces weighted disproportionately against their organized strength, and Nkrumah became the sole and central political figure personifying not only the CPP and all that it represented but, more importantly, also the movement of the black race toward emancipation from external domination and subjugation. He caused his image to be imprinted onto the new postindependence coins (shillings and pence) of Ghana. It must be hurriedly stated that the prime minister failed to have his image similarly printed on the currency notes because he was opposed by his finance minister, Mr. K. A. Gbedemah, who did not want any effigy on the currency at all and therefore resigned his post in protest. As a compromise to win his able finance minister back, Nkrumah capitulated and limited the imprint on the coins only. The CPP, being rendered amorphous by the dominance of the personality of its leader, in turn became the breeding grounds for a horde of sycophants who only pandered to the whims of the leader.

It was in this state of affairs that the other groups came together to form a nominal "united party," after the Preventive Detention Act (PDA) had effectively crippled[10] them. Under the PDA, the imminent threat of being imprisoned without trial hung over the head of anyone who said too much or acted too much in contradiction of the ideological and political lines of Nkrumah and the CPP. Many well-meaning citizens fled abroad into exile. The courts and judicial officers became helpless appendages to a new aberration of justice, themselves being subjected to the tyranny of the CPP and its leader. This situation prevailed until the twenty-fourth of February 1966, when postindependence Ghana had the first coup d'état and Africa, south of the Sahara, experienced the third (the first being in Togo in January 1963 when then Sergeant Étienne Eyadéma ousted President Sylvanus Olympio in a very bloody coup, the second being in Nigeria in December 1965) in a series of military interventions in African constitutional dispensations.

---

10   The enactment of the Preventive Detection Act (PDA) and its abuses.

CHAPTER SEVEN

THE POLITICAL SCENE OF 1966-1992

The Military Intervention of the National Liberation Council

Empirically, it would appear that a people deserve the type of government they have got, and a tyrant is a construct of his own people. After the 1966 coup d'état (this writer has no knowledge as to the operations of the CIA and no evidence that the coup of 1966 was supported or aided or sponsored by the CIA), the political leadership of Ghana was obsessed with ascertaining the circumstances necessitating the staging of the coup. This obsession in turn created quite unreasonable hysteria at any mention of the name of Nkrumah or the CPP. The National Liberation Council (NLC), the military regime that supplanted the "elected" CPP government, committed a number of mistakes springing directly from its intolerance and antagonism toward any individuals who were even remotely or historically linked to the former government. Moreover, the NLC conducted its affairs as if it had no vision or purpose, save that it came to topple a dictatorship, in which case, it should not have hung on to power. It behaved just like a group of soldiers and their police collaborators who overthrew a set of politicians in government just to replace them exclusively with the ousted government's political opponents. Furthermore, the general populace began to discern and complain about a number of the characteristics of the new military government, especially its composition and attitude regarding ethnocentrism and tribalism.

First, there emerged an anti-Ewe feeling among sections of the populace of non-Voltaic stock because of the preponderant Ewe-dominated membership of the ruling military junta. Secondly, on the seventeenth of April 1967, there was a countercoup. Although it was foiled, General Ankrah, head of state and chairman of the NLC, had to take cover and was saved. However, General E. K. Kotoka was killed. After one afternoon's news bulletin on Radio Ghana a few days prior to the April 17 incident, Dr. K. A. Busia aired a public pronouncement as follows: "Those who seize power were often not agreed on the composition of the government or policies of their regime. This often results in counter coups and in some cases shootings at their meetings." This was an important statement from an equally important member and political adviser to the military junta, which most likely was made on the premise of firsthand observation, experience, and knowledge.

Thirdly, after a radio announcement by one Major Sowu in the wake of the April 17 abortive coup, to the effect that "the attempted counter coup has been foiled" and only after the dead and mutilated body of General Kotoka had been found in the bushes near the Accra international airport, the whereabouts of Dr. K. A. Busia and Colonel Akwasi Amankwaa Afrifa were reported to be at Dormaa Ahenkro on the Ghana-Côte d'Ivoire border and Bawku on the Ghana-Burkina Faso border respectively. These queer coincidences and the subsequent ouster of Lieutenant General J. A. Ankrah in a Joseph Arthur Francis Nzeribe scandal raised suspicions, rightly or wrongly, of a deliberate implementation of a campaign of intrigue, whose nature was colored with tribalism and ethnocentrism. It should be noted that the initial composition of the NLC was as follows: Lieutenant General J. A. Ankrah, head of state and commander in chief of the Ghana Armed Forces (a Ga), as chairman; Mr. J. W. K. Harley, IGP (an Ewe), as deputy chairman; Major General Emmanuel Kwasi Kotoka, general officer commanding the Ghana Armed Forces (an Ewe), member; Brigadier A. K. Ocran (a Fanti), member; Mr. A. K. Deku, COP CID (an Ewe), member; Mr. E. O. Nunoo, commissioner of police administration (a Ga), member; Colonel A. A. Afrifa (an Asante), member; and Mr. B. A. Yakubu, deputy commissioner of police (a Northerner), member. In addition, Mr. Victor Owusu and Dr. K. A. Busia were the attorney general and political adviser respectively of the military junta.

Fourthly, the Constitution on which the conduct and results of the 1969 general elections were based and which disqualified Busia's main opponent, K. A. Gbedemah, without proving any criminal conduct against him, had an ephemeral existence. The mass dismissal of public servants (in which the figure 568 was given as the number affected, evidently economized on the truth) and the poor or bad execution of an otherwise patriotic policy that led to the forcible deportation of "aliens" en masse exacerbated the feeling of tribal and/or ethnic persecution. The government persistently refused to publish any lists of the affected people at all, and the general perception was that the dismissals were designed against and targeted at Ewes. But this policy proved to be costly for the second Republican government led by Busia since the mass dismissals, if at all, succeeded in depleting the civil service of vital middle- and higher-level managerial and administrative manpower, which seriously affected the quality of operation of government machinery. In fact, these acts were an indictment of a government that had sworn to uphold the Constitution, which protected and guaranteed the fundamental rights of citizens.

In fact, a manager of the erstwhile Ghana National Trading Corporation (GNTC), Mr. Sallah, one of the government employees affected by the mass dismissals, did sue the government of Ghana and got judgment in his favour. Anticipating and fearing the floodgate of lawsuits that the Sallah judgment would throw open, the prime minister, Dr. K. A. Busia, went on public radio and television to criticize the judgment. In the course of his speech, Dr. Busia made the following emotional outburst: "No court. No court; I say no court can coerce my government to employ anybody." Some political commentators and observers are of the opinion that Busia's overthrow was a direct result of this outburst against the decision of the court. Others, too, insist that it was the result of a badly implemented bad policy. So that having regard to all the facts and circumstances, the judgment will not be perverse to say that the mother of all the military takeovers subsequent to the 1966 coup d'état in Ghana was Busia's influence, methods, policies, and governance.

Ghana under the NRC/SMC Rule—the Undoing of Military Interventionism

The most justifiable grounds for forcibly removing the Progress Party government of Dr. Busia in 1972, which incidentally also reflected the public perception at the time, as contained in the announcement of Colonel Ignatius Kutu Acheampong, was that "people were exposed to the dangers of destruction through massive hunger and pain, and the government deliberately embark upon a programme of removing bread from the mouth of the people through arbitrary dismissal from employment and policies aimed at widening the circle of poverty." It was as if the new military junta was sending the message that it was not that people did not know rules but it is that when people are forced into desperation, when people do not feel safe in their own country anymore, to preach virtuous conduct will be to no avail because the propensity to be virtuous will be absent and rules will be broken since people would be more predisposed to do so. Ironically, this was the general atmosphere in the country under the rule of Colonel I. K. Acheampong and his National Redemption Council (NRC). Just a few years after leading a military coup to overthrow the government and suspend the short-lived 1969 Second Republican Constitution, the country's economy took a steep nose-dive from 1975, resulting in widespread hunger and deprivation on an unprecedented scale. The law of the jungle in which the fittest survived was the order of the day: corruption was on an unimaginable scale and had seeped from the corridors of power and authority into the last strands of the fabric of society.

The main characteristic of this widespread cancer was the indiscriminate cheating and profiteering that gave birth to the term *Kalabuley*. Women suddenly rose in economic importance and dominated trade and commerce, taking advantage of their gender and association with men in power and public authority. Public shop shelves became bare, while hoarding of the very scarce consumer commodities and profiteering on them bred the generation of the bold and daring "briefcase businessmen," whose burgeoning "middleman" business was transacted from briefcases they totted around and not from any established business address. Nepotism and cronyism thrived under these conditions, and the machinery of state and law and order could not withstand the weight of the piling pressures. Visible cracks began to show in the brittle governing military regime. The commissions, omissions, and governance ineptitude of the military junta had all culminated in loss of purpose and general anarchy: the people began to lose confidence in government and its political leaders.

Acheampong, too, resorted to intrigue, systematically removing the people who had initially helped to catapult him to power by overthrowing Busia in 1972, but this did not improve matters. Later, in a desperate bid to maintain himself in power in the face of huge political, economic, and social odds, Acheampong attempted to introduce a novel type of government that he called union government, after changing the name of the NRC to the Supreme Military Council (SMC). However, this was only diversionary and meant to sway public attention from the serious social confusion and crisis in the national economy. Acheampong had become, indeed, helpless.

It began to dawn on some members of the SMC that the prevailing situation in the country was eroding the image of the armed forces at large and subjecting them individually and collectively to disgrace and public odium. It was not surprising, therefore, when a bloodless palace coup was executed against General Acheampong, led by General Frank William K. Akuffo, his next in command. The SMC II thus came into being in 1979. But by this time, the image of the armed forces had been battered badly. In fact, the image of the armed forces had sagged to its lowest ebb in the estimation of the general public to the extent that the junior officers found it necessary to rebel against their commanders, whom they saw as corrupt and insincere.

When Flight Lieutenant John Jerry Rawlings and his Armed Forces Revolutionary Council (AFRC) mutinied and executed their senior officers, they were actually venting their anger and frustration as soldiers about what they perceived to be the disgrace that their commanders, among other things, had brought onto the armed forces. This would explain the military putsch of May 15, 1979, and the uprising on June 4, 1979, in the armed forces, which events thrust Flight Lieutenant Rawlings from a hitherto obscure existence into the limelight of national politics. But then it is merely prospective to speculate whether or not the revolution on December 31, 1981, would have taken place if Flight Lieutenant Rawlings and the retired Captain Kojo Tsikata had not suffered harassment from government security agencies after conducting elections and handing over power to Dr. Hilla Limann's government. Therefore, a discussion of that issue will not be attempted here. However, there is sufficient evidence to show that Captain Tsikata had indeed suffered harassment in the form of overt surveillance of his movements. This was by the national security agencies during the Limann administration and also under Dr. Busia's Progress Party government, even though he is not known to be a part of the coup that toppled Dr. Busia from power in 1972.

In any case, both the retired captain and J. J. Rawlings were part of the vanguard of the military overthrow of the legitimate People's National Party (PNP) government in the coup on December 31, 1981, just a little over two years after the AFRC had handed over power to Dr. Limann's third Republican government. The short stay of Rawlings and the AFRC in power (about three months) was unprecedented in the history of coups, especially in Africa. This, coupled with their ability to organize a relatively free and fair general election to usher in a constitutional government, had transmuted whatever excesses and shortcomings of the junta and its leader into acts of patriotism, in the estimation of citizens, in view of the national situation before the mutiny.

PNDC Era in Perspective—Crucible for Rebirth of Democracy and Constitutionality

The coup of December 31, 1981, like all coups that topple legitimate constitutionality, is distasteful and must always be condemned and discouraged. It curtails the development and/or evolution of the exercise of the free will by the people in the development of a system of government that provides and guarantees for them freedoms and security to their persons and property. This system has its own inbuilt checks and balances to curb arbitrariness and excesses on the part of any branch of government, and the people themselves determine who represent their interests in decision-making. All these ideals cannot be manifested under a military rule, no matter what its pretensions to adherence to any patriotic or democratic ideals, because the coup and its makers usurp the inalienable rights and privileges of the people to freely decide their own destinies and the rule by fiat and decree replace free competition of ideas.

Patriotism is inclusive but is never also altruistic. In his actions, a patriot contemplates his own benefits as well as that of others in a system; otherwise, his acts would tend to be perfunctory, and a perfunctory act is not a desirable act. It is the duty and obligation of every patriotic citizen to help make his/her country stable, great, and prosperous. It is, however, abstruse to classify a coup maker as a patriot. A true patriot would not subvert the very reasons for his claim to be a patriot. A coup maker uses the force of arms to seize power from a legitimate, constitutional government elected by the free will of the people. In the process, he maims, kills, or otherwise destroys others, for when he succeeds in his adventure, he becomes an idol of the society, and when he fails, he is condemned.

The Provisional National Defense Council, or the PNDC as it came to be better known, was the most controversial, paradoxical, and longest-ruling military government in the history of Ghana. In the first place, it disguised itself as a nonmilitary administration by filling its ruling council and government positions largely with civilian appointees. But its ties to and reliance on the military as the real power base was very palpable, visible, and omnipresent. It replaced and, in most cases, supplanted vital formal institutional function with what was described as "people's power": People's Tribunals began to function and dispense "instant justice"; People's Defense Committees became the de facto custodians of legislative and executive powers from grassroots to the national level, in the communities, and at places of work. The inexperience of the people's power operatives and the overenthusiastic application of the vast discretionary powers at their disposal sooner than later began to exact its toll on the national economy and the public psyche.

A culture of silence was borne out of fear of victimization if one was not careful enough about what one said or did. Instant justice was meted out gleefully by members of the armed forces and police on one hand, and members of the Defense Committees was the order of the day. Public flogging of even women and some other forms of debasing treatment were meted out upon the flimsiest accusation without proper investigation or inquiry. The overzealous pursuit of "probity and accountability" turned virtually into a witch hunt. Available stocks of consumer commodities were sold out at "controlled prices." The ensuing shortages due to the inability to import goods to replenish depleted stocks owing to foreign exchange constraints led to the harassment and persecution of persons with any quantities of consumer items for hoarding, with immediate and inevitable consequences. People were tried before People's Tribunals and executed by firing squad or jailed for corruption. Factories and assets of individuals were confiscated for alleged tax evasion etc. In consequence, some investors fled the country, while none were eager to come to invest in the national economy. Industrial production output began to dwindle, and the scarce foreign exchange, which was available, had to be used to import produce that were once produced locally.

Following a spell of drought, a general food shortage resulting in hunger in the early 1980s exacerbated the suffering of Ghanaians. An energy crisis that saw the first load shedding and power rationing that sent industrial production reeling further did not help the situation. Several attempts at economic recovery were made. Initially, the response from the Breton Wood institutions was negative, apparently owing to the socialist leanings and rhetoric of the PNDC. In the face of the deepening economic crisis, the regime shifted tack and began responding to demands by donor and lending institutions for structural adjustment conditional to obtaining loan and other facilities to finance national economic recovery. Overall, the economy did not fare very well under the better part of the rule of the PNDC, but there began to emerge a tentative movement toward institutional reforms and practice that bode well for future democratic practice.

Some of the more positive legacies from the PNDC era are the very foundations upon which the fourth republic and longest-running democratic dispensation has been constructed. Indeed, the novelty of the District Assembly system of decentralized governance is yet the most unique contribution of Ghana and Africa to the global democratization process. It started with an attempt to develop the Defense Committee structures into People's Assemblies from the community through District Assemblies up to a National Assembly by representation of the people by the people. The underlying principle was borrowed from the Libyan Jamahiriyya representation of the people model. Furthermore, it is significant and quite important to note that the PNDC set into motion the process that has produced one of the finest examples of a stable African democratic nationhood, highlighting tenacity in its adherence to democratic ideals in spite of the country's recent history of turbulent military intervention. A Consultative Assembly of Eminent Persons was set up in 1990 to draft the Fourth Republican Constitution—a constitution that has survived four successive governments with two four-year terms each so far, with the first ever smooth transfer of power from one elected government to another after generally fair and free elections. This feat is rare in the history of Africa and the Third World and wherever the military have come in direct contact with political power. The novelty about the Constitution of the Fourth Republic of Ghana lies in its blend of the Westminster and United States of America constitutional frameworks—a blend that has proved to be rather challenging in governance.

It is sufficiently demonstrated that the military have used various reasons, especially that of abuse of constitutional powers vested in leaders of governments, to justify and rationalize their illegal intervention in the democratic process. It has also been shown that the military have brought nothing but misery and negative development to Ghana and anywhere else they have come into government. Therefore, the question is posed, Is it innate weaknesses in the Constitution that enable constitutionally elected governments to misgovern and thus provide the excuse for military intervention, or is it structural weaknesses in the constitutional framework and its institutions established to aid the democratic process that is to blame? To encapsulate the question, one may ask, What type of constitution or, better, what guarantees must be provided in the constitution such that it would become unattractive for the military to invade and take over the democratic process and such that governments would find it practically impossible to digress into pursuit of their own whims and caprices?

Certainly, we need a constitution under which worthy, able-bodied, and patriotic citizens of Ghana can fashion their affairs in such a way as to contribute to the reduction and possible eradication of poverty and illiteracy, to obliterate ignorance through innovative and advanced tuition and learning methods that will expose the best potential in each citizen and bring it to bear on national advancement.

We need a constitution that will not repose in any individual or group of individuals any sweeping discretionary powers without any checks at all. It is thus proposed now to critically examine the landmark provisions in the Constitution of the Fourth Republic of Ghana, which came into effect in 1992. This is with the view not just to inform or, for that matter, equip ourselves with necessary knowledge to safeguard our own interests as citizens and to be better equipped to defend the same Constitution with all our strength and with all our will as good patriots of the land but more so to seek conscientiously to refine the same Constitution in order that it may serve our collective interests and aspirations all the better.

It is proposed to discuss the provisions analytically and not merely descriptively. As we proceed, it will be instructive to well consider the following prologue:

> Political freedom is possible only where justice is in the seat of authority; where all orders and decrees work in harmony with organic laws, which man neither made himself nor can alter or manipulate to do injustice; where those who are trusted with power use it in fairness to all for the common good. Where justice is supreme, no subject is forbidden anything, which he has a right to do or to desire. Therefore, political change, revolutions, reforms, transfers, etc. are themselves not necessary

indications of political or moral advance. Empirically, healthy nations, when justly governed, never demand constitutional changes. The need is to avoid the abuse of political power and privileges for personal advantage or for public mischief.

Chapter Eight

THE PROVISIONS OF THE CONSTITUTION OF THE REPUBLIC OF GHANA (1992)

General Provisions

The provisions of the Constitution of the Republic of Ghana (1992) are such that this Constitution can be described as a landmark constitution for a number of reasons. The first and quite remarkable thing to note is that there is no preamble to the provisions, unlike the previous Republican or independence constitutions where the preamble of those constitutions addressed all the needs that would enable or oblige the state to ensure that justice, freedom, and liberty of the citizen is recognized and accorded to every citizen. But when the enforcement of the contents of the preamble was sought in court,[11] the expatriate attorney general of the first republic, Geoffrey Bing, argued that the preamble did not form part of the Constitution, and therefore, the court did not have any power to order its enforcement. The court upheld this argument and dismissed the habeas corpus application of the citizens. The result was that the applicants were kept in detention without trial until some of them died within prison confinement, like J. B. Danquah, while others were rendered blind at the

---

11   In Re Akoto and others.

time they were released after, as stated before, the second coup in Sub-Saharan Africa in 1966.

It is therefore refreshing that the 1992 Constitution of the Republic of Ghana has recognized and asserted, by itself, that the people of Ghana are sovereign under the Almighty God to exercise their natural and inalienable right to establish their own framework of government. The assertion of Ghanaians reads:

IN THE NAME OF THE ALMIGHTY GOD. We the people of Ghana, IN EXERCISE of our natural and inalienable right to establish a framework of government which shall secure for ourselves and posterity the blessing, liberty, equality of opportunity and prosperity; AND IN SOLEMN declaration and affirmation of our commitment to Freedom, Justice, Probity and Accountability; The principle that all powers of government spring from the sovereign will of the people; The principle of Universal Adult Suffrage; The Rule of Law; The protection and preservation Fundamental Human Rights and Freedoms, Unity, and Stability; DO HEREBY ADOPT, ENACT AND GIVE TO OURSELVES THIS CONSTITUTION.

Under this solemn resolve, it should be possible for the superior courts of judicature not to allow or condone or encourage any legal ingenuity any time to rubbish the immutable responsibility on the president under Articles 34–40 in Chapter 6 of the Constitution, "which enjoins the President to deliver at least once a year to Parliament, an address on the state of the nation." It is envisaged that the president, in complying with Section 34 (2), will have to address the Parliament, adverting to all the requirements stipulated under the Directive Principles of State Policy, after which time there must be a critical discussion of the report of the president on the state of the nation as required. It is submitted that this provision places the president of Ghana in a similar position as the president of the

United States of America, who is annually required in the same vein to deliver the State of the Union Address.

The Territories of Ghana

1. Citizenship and the Laws of Ghana

The State of Ghana is a sovereign unitary republic comprising the territories in the regions existing before the coming into force of this Constitution. Parliament may make law for the delimitation of the country's territorial, sea space, and various zones. And the president may create a new region or regions by altering the existing boundaries by mergers if there is any petition to that effect and on the advice of the Council of State or even if there is no petition but the Council of State advises on the need for creating a new region. The rationale being that the state and its regions cannot remain static when there is a growth of population or any development that may require adjustment in any of the existing regions for the smooth and/or economic administration of the state. However, the president does not exercise absolute or discretionary power in respect to merging or altering the boundaries of the regions. Article 5 of the Constitution clearly regulates the president's power. The president becomes satisfied on the advice of the Council of State, and in some respects, the president has to appoint a Commission of Inquiry into the demand. And if the recommendation of the commission so appointed is favorable and the Council of State so advises, the president will refer the matter to the Electoral Commission and specify thereto questions to be answered in a referendum. It is envisaged that stability needs to be maintained in the regions to obviate any capricious or whimsical action to satisfy purely sectional interests (3).

2. Citizenship of Ghana

The chapter on citizenship is a bit bogging. At the time Article 8 of the Constitution was amended, it was not deemed necessary to remove the word *birth* from Article 6 (3) in Chapter 3 of the Constitution. Indeed, the word *birth* appears only four times throughout the provisions. It first occurs in Article 6 (2) and (3) and then in 9 (3) and 62 (a). But for the word *birth* in these articles, the constitutional provisions on citizenship would appear as enlightened and straightforward provision for liberalism and progress. The word *birth* therefore serves as the pinch of salt that has spoiled the broth.

This Constitution does not define citizenship by birth in respect to people born before the Constitution came into force. But by Article 62 (a), a person shall not qualify for election as the president of Ghana unless he is a "citizen by birth." However, the only definition of who is a citizen by birth can be found in Article 6 (3), which provides that "a child not more than seven years of age found in Ghana whose parents are not known shall be presumed to be a citizen of Ghana by birth." So in effect, no person who was born before this Constitution came into effect can be a citizen of Ghana by birth under the Constitution, except a foundling. It is hereby therefore humbly suggested that Articles 6 (3), 9 (3), and 62 (a) should be amended by deleting the phrase "by birth" therefrom to read in 6 (3) "A child not more than seven years of age found in Ghana whose parents are not known shall be presumed to be a citizen of Ghana" and by replacing the phrase "otherwise than by birth" in 9 (3) with the words "by naturalization or registration" and 62 to read "A person shall not be qualified for election as the President of Ghana unless: [a] he is a citizen of Ghana."

On the other hand, as it is improper that a dual citizen or citizen by registration should become the president of Ghana, it should be so stated explicitly. Then whenever anyone or a group of people finds it necessary to object to an individual's desire to be elected as president of Ghana, it will then become a matter for the laws of the land as legitimized under Article 11 of the Constitution. Perhaps there is the need to take a cue from neighboring Côte d'Ivoire and to avert a repetition of the fundamental mistake of unclear constitutional definition of citizenship, especially where it has to do with ascent to political office such as the presidency.

3. Fundamental Human Rights and Freedoms

The most striking provision relating to fundamental human rights and freedoms are Articles 2 (1) (a) and (b) and 17 of the Constitution. When these articles are taken together and alongside Article 12 of Chapter 5 on human rights and freedoms, the ordinary citizen or the common man can be assured that there are safeguards for his fair treatment. What is next is for him to be aware of his rights. Article 2 (1) (b) provides as follows:

> 2 (1) A person who alleges that
>
> (a) An enactment or anything contained or done under the authority of that or any other enactment; or
>
> (b) Any act or omission of any person is inconsistent with, or is in contravention of the provision of this Constitution, may bring an action in the Supreme Court for a declaration to that effect.
>
> (2) The Supreme Court shall, for the purposes of a declaration under clause (1) of this Article, make such orders and give such direction as it may consider appropriate for giving effect, or enabling effect to be given, to the declaration so made.
>
> (3) Any person or group of persons to whom an order or direction is addressed under clause 2 of this Article by the Supreme Court, shall duly obey and carry out the terms of the order or direction.
>
> (4) Failure to obey or carry out the terms of an order or direction made or given under clause 2 of this Article constitutes a high crime under this Constitution and shall, in the case of the President or the Vice-President, constitute grounds for removal from office under this Constitution.
>
> (5) A person convicted of a high crime under clause 4 of this Article shall:
>
> (a) Be liable to imprisonment for not exceeding ten years without the option of a fine; and
>
> (b) Not be eligible for election or for appointment, to any public office for ten years beginning with the expiry of the term of imprisonment".

Article 12 provides that the fundamental rights and freedoms enshrined in this chapter (Chapter 5) on human rights and freedoms shall be respected and upheld by the executive, the legislative, and the judiciary and all other organs of government and its agencies and all natural and legal persons in Ghana, where applicable to them, and shall be enforceable by the courts as provided for in this Constitution. And every person in Ghana—whatever his race, place of origin, political opinion, skin colour, religion, creed, or gender—shall be entitled to the fundamental human rights and freedoms of the individual contained in this chapter but subject to respect for the rights and freedoms of others and for the public interest.

Article 17 provides that all persons shall be equal before the law and a person shall not be discriminated against on the grounds of gender, race, colour, ethnic origin, religion, creed, or social or economic status. And the Constitution defines the word *discriminate* for the purpose of Article 17 as "to give different treatment to different persons attributable only or mainly to their respective descriptions by race, place of origin, political opinions, colour, gender, occupation, religion or creed whereby persons of one description are subjected to disabilities or restrictions to which persons of another description are not made subject, or are granted privileges and advantages which are not granted to persons of another description." However, there is a requirement, it would appear, that there should be a demarcation or distinction between the Article 2 position requiring action in the Supreme Court and the Articles 12–33 position empowering an aggrieved person to sue in the High Court. Although both provisions ultimately have the effect of enforcing people's rights and the Constitution, the two situations should not be confused or blurred. While the Article 2 provision would basically appear to be concerned with construction or interpretation of the Constitution in the Supreme Court, the Articles 12–33 provisions deal with the fundamental rights remedies in the High Court. Thus, any legal action arising from complaints in the nature of Article 17 of the Constitution does not have to be in the Supreme Court. The proper forum would be the High Court. It thus appears that the Article 2 provision is referable to the Directive Principles of State Policy grave issues that touch on the Constitution itself.

4. *The Directive Principles of State Policy*

The Directive Principles of State Policy found in Articles 34–40 (Chapter 6) of the Constitution are meant to animate every policy of government and guide every state organ—president, Cabinet members of the National Assembly (Parliament) and the judiciary, etc.—in policy formulation and execution throughout Ghana. They are the ultimate ideals set down to be met by the state and its organs. While the state is equated with the president, in his functions as head of state in these ideals, Article 41 enjoins every citizen in reciprocation to show utmost patriotism and responsible behaviour in all things and everywhere as Ghanaians. And by Article 34 (2), "The President shall report once in a year all the steps taken to ensure the realization of the policy objectives contained in this Chapter; and, in particular, the realization of basic human rights, a healthy economy, the right to work, the right to good healthcare and the right to education."

It may be trite to state that the extent of the realization of the Directive Principles of State Policy will be the function of the caliber of the citizenry, which will include the facultative quality of the citizenry. This will in turn depend on the environment within which the citizen's faculty is manifested. This is because a very good system that is entrusted to bad people will be badly executed while a system not so good but entrusted into the hands of good people will be managed to some good effect. That is the essence of the Directive Principles of State Policy, which, by and large, cannot be enforced by any legal action in the courts, save Parliament's critical evaluation of the president's report to Parliament and the personnel serving with the government.

1. In Re Akoto and others.
2. Chapter 6 of constitution on Article 67.
3. Articles 4 and 5.

CHAPTER NINE

THE LEGISLATIVE, THE EXECUTIVE, AND THE JUDICIARY

The Legislative

The Parliament of Ghana comprises 175 members of a single House elected by 175 constituencies. Every normal citizen who is eighteen years of age is qualified to vote for a member of Parliament, but to be voted for as a member of Parliament, a candidate must have attained the age of twenty-one (6) years and must not be a dual citizen or bankrupt under any law in force in Ghana etc. Membership of Parliament is a full-time occupation during the member's tenure. The validity of the election of a member of Parliament and that of the speaker are subject to the jurisdiction of the High Court (7). The full details of membership, operations, and privileges of Parliament can be found under Articles 95–124 (Chapter 10) of the Constitution.

Representation of the People (Election of Members of Parliament)

It has been noted that there are two age limits for electoral purposes. To qualify to vote, a Ghanaian must attain eighteen years of age and be registered as a voter. In order to be voted for to become a member of Parliament, twenty-one years is the age limit. These are basic qualifications or requirements for a voter and a candidate respectively. All matters pertaining to elections and referenda in the country are the responsibility of the Electoral Commission.

The commission comprises (a) a chairman, (b) two deputy chairmen, and (c) four other members who are appointed under Article 70 of the Constitution. While the chairman of the Electoral Commission has the status and conditions of service equivalent to that of a justice of the Court of Appeal, the other two deputies have the status and conditions of service equivalent to High Court judges, and they are not permitted to hold any other public office simultaneously. The other four members of the commission are paid allowances such as are determined by Parliament. The following are the responsibilities of the Electoral Commission:

a.   Compilation and periodic revision of the register of voters
b.   Demarcation of electoral boundaries for both national and local government elections
c.   The conduct and supervision of all public elections and referenda
d.   Education of the public on the electoral process and its purpose
e.   Undertaking the formulation of programmes for revision and/or expansion of the voters' register
f.   The performance of functions as may be prescribed by law

The commission is an independent organ of the state apparatus and not subject to the direction or control of any other person or authority. The commission carries out its functions by dividing the country into constituencies for the purpose of electing members of Parliament such that no constituency shall fall within more than one region. The commission divides the population by the number of constituencies for every constituency to be a "population quota" or a little more or less of that quota for administrative convenience. For every public election or referendum, voting shall be by secret ballot, and immediately after the close of the poll, the ballot papers shall be counted right there at the polling station and recorded and announced to the people present. This is to forestall any doctoring of the results after leaving the polling station (8) so that the chances for securing the true and real choices of the electorate in any election can be guaranteed.

Political Parties

By Article 3 (1), "Parliament shall have no power to enact a law establishing a one party state." It is therefore certain that political parties are a necessary component part of the country's system of government. Thus, any individual can originate or form a political party. So also, every person is free to join any political party. However, political parties are barred from sponsoring candidates for election into local government district assemblies or other lower local government units. This notwithstanding, a political party shall have a national character. There must be founding members in all the regions of the country, and every founding member must be a qualified registered voter. A person who is not qualified to vote cannot be a founding member of a political party. Every party must be registered with the Electoral Commission and must provide the names and addresses of the founding members of the party. Political parties must also declare their assets and the sources of their assets to the public. The members of the National Executive Committee of every political party must be chosen from all the regions of Ghana. In addition, the state media are enjoined to give equal airtime to all presidential candidates to present their programmes to the electorate and general public.

The Executive

The Presidency and the Council of State

Under the Republican Constitution of 1992, the executive powers and functions of the country are vested in the president and his Cabinet as assisted by the Council of State in its advisory capacity (10). The president is the head of state and commander in chief of the Armed Forces of Ghana. While holding office, the president leaves the shores of Ghana only after signing by himself a notification to that effect addressed to the speaker of Parliament. For the duration of his tenure of office, the president enjoys immunity from all legal actions and liability, whether civil or criminal, and this immunity continues as regards personal acts or omissions before or during his term of office notwithstanding any period of limitation, except where the proceedings had been barred before he assumed office as president. The president takes precedence in Ghana before any other person and before the vice president and speaker of Parliament and the chief justice. However, in the absence of the president from Ghana, the vice president performs the functions of the president (11) after he has taken the appropriate oath in the Second Schedule to the Constitution.

The vice president is normally elected on the same day and platform as the president. It is a constitutional requirement that during the electioneering campaign, the presidential candidate for each political party must designate a candidate as his running mate for vice president prior to the election. This is highly ideal and desirable as a check against dictatorship. Thus, while in office and if the president and vice president should have a serious misunderstanding or reservation over any issue or issues, the president has no power to remove his vice or appoint another person of his choice to replace him. This arrangement serves as an effective check and balance of power. It would appear that the only obvious or sensible thing to do in the event of a disagreement or stalemate over an issue between the president and his vice is to call for a presidential election.

The mode of electing the president is set out in Article 63, and if a challenge against his election should be successful, it is considered as against both the president and vice president. On assuming office as the president of the Republic of Ghana, the president becomes vested with enormous executive powers.

The Cabinet

The Cabinet comprises the president, vice president, and not less than ten or more than nineteen ministers of state with a secretary to the Cabinet all appointed by the president. By Article 78 (3), a minister of state shall not hold any other office of profit or emolument, whether private or public and whether directly or indirectly, unless permitted by the speaker of Parliament on certain grounds. Subject to the discretion of the president, Articles 78–82 regulate the tenure of a member of the Cabinet.

From the point of view of corporate governance, the Cabinet represents the governing or executive council of government business with the president as its chief executive. It is therefore both an agenda-setting body and executor of policies. It has to achieve specific targets not only dictated by constitutional provisions but also by the vision of the president and his sponsoring political party for the development of the country. Toward the achievement of these goals, the president and the Cabinet are assisted by and work through the agency of some specialized commissions and bodies that are accountable directly to the president.

The National Security Council

There is a National Security Council that is presided over by the president himself. It comprises the president, the vice president, and eight ex officio members who are members of the National Security Council by virtue of the positions they hold as public officers. However, the president may invite such other persons he considers necessary for any deliberations of the council. But invited participants, in such circumstances, cannot vote on any issues in the deliberations. The secretary to the Cabinet is also the secretary to the National Security Council. The National Security Council is also responsible for safeguarding the internal and external security of the state (12).

The National Development Planning Commission

The National Development Planning Commission comprises a chairman who is appointed by the president in consultation with the Council of State and the minister of finance, government statistician, and governor of the Bank of Ghana as ex officio members. There is also one representative from each region appointed by the Regional Coordinating Council and such other persons as may be appointed by the president under Article 86 (2) (vi). The National Development Planning Commission is responsible to the president, and its function is to advise the president on development planning policy and strategy (13).

The Attorney General

The Constitution does not say everything about the attorney general. The office of an attorney general is not an enviable one. The office has both common law functions and statutory powers, and the attorney general has legal as well as ministerial functions. The attorney general is the principal legal adviser to the government, and he has responsibility to discharge other legal functions assigned to him by the president. As the principal legal adviser of the government, the attorney general may have other legal functions imposed on him by the Constitution and any other law. For example, as the minister of justice, he has ministerial responsibility for all matters affecting the judiciary.

In hierarchy, the office of the attorney general ranks higher than that of a High Court judge. Upon assumption of office, the attorney general becomes the leader of the bar of his country. He normally should have his own patriotic vision and yet he has to tow the line of the government whose attorney general he is. The office of the attorney general is therefore unique among the other ministers. The attorney general has to discharge such other duties of legal nature as may be referred or assigned to him by the president; he is responsible for initiation and conduct of all criminal prosecutions and institution and conduct of all civil cases on behalf of the state. All civil litigations against the state are instituted against the attorney general as defendant. There are certain prosecutions that can only serve as embarrassment to the government and certain civil claims against the government that may constitute problems for the state. In all such situations, the attorney general must find solutions and advise government on the possible ways out.

As the leader of the bar of his country, the attorney general must normally listen and consider the stance of his colleagues at the bar on major issues, and yet he has to offer considered legal advice to the government. So in a number of circumstances where there is conflict, he has to consider whether to remain in office or to resign. Thus, and unlike a judicial officer whose function is purely judicial, the position of the attorney general is both political and legal. He sometimes also has quasi-judicial decisions to make. In this position, the attorney general has some discretionary powers at common law. One of these discretionary powers is to enter nolle prosequi in criminal prosecutions. The attorney general can enter a nolle prosequi in any criminal proceeding at any stage of the matter, and he is not obliged to give any reasons for doing so. Whenever his advice is not acceptable to the government, he may only resign or the government may relieve him of the position of attorney general.

Throughout the common law world—Britain, Canada, Australia, United States of America, and other stable democracies—military regimes have not been known. Thus, the institution of attorney general is a common law institution, and it functions in democratic settings under the rule of law. Now:

i.   The conditions that prevailed during Dr. Kwame Nkrumah's Ghana were not democratic. This cannot be validly denied. Therefore, Mr. Geoffrey Bing, the attorney general, did not operate in a democratic setting when he acted for his government in the case of In Re Akoto and others.

ii.   The conduct of Mr. Akinjide, federal attorney general of Nigeria in 1979.

iii.   When Obasanjo was to hand over power as a military ruler to an elected civilian government in 1979, none of Nigeria's presidential candidates scored the required two-thirds of the nineteen states forming the Nigerian federation that year. Instead of following the constitutional requirement for holding a run-up election between the two best candidates, Obasanjo feared that the dreaded Awolowo-led government would come into power. Obasanjo's military regime decided to hand over power to Shehu Shagari. In order to succeed in that, Obasanjo instructed his attorney general to go to court to thwart the Nigerian electoral system under the 1979 Constitution, and Akinjide, the attorney general, complied. During the proceedings in court, a subpoena was issued to a professor of mathematics from the University of Lagos (Prof. Chike Obi) to appear in court for a calculation of two-thirds of nineteen states, and in the end, the Nigerian

Supreme Court ridiculed itself in the eyes of the world. This was during a military regime and not under a democracy.

iv. Again, the performance of the attorney general of Lagos State in the case involving the death of Dele Giwa, a journalist who was killed by a parcel bomb suspected to have been delivered from the seat of the security outfit under the military regime of Ibrahim Babangida, in which the Lagos State attorney general was said to have deliberately bungled the case and got it thrown out of court, was during military dictatorship.

v. The brutal murders of the three High Court judges and a retired major of the Ghana Army, where the attorney general, under the regime of the PNDC, rejected some of the recommendations of the Special Investigation Board (SIB), rightly or wrongly occurred during the rule of an extraordinary military regime and not in a democratic setting.

Each of all these attorneys general was exercising the discretionary power of an attorney general as it is known. Since all the foregoing performances took place under circumstances that cannot be described as democratic or under the rule of law, it will be wrong to use those abnormalities as the basis for measuring the proper functions of the attorney general in any constitutional arrangement. Therefore, it will be perverse to jettison the functions of the attorney general in any democratic setting, using any of those instances, without any proper or workable alternative institution to obtain constitutionalism. There should not be any hasty attempt to jettison the institution of the attorney general in any constitutional arrangement or act in a manner that can create any intractable condition. To do so will rather produce serious negative results, which will impair democracy and the rule of law.

What is needed now is to throw away the evils of the past and forge ahead in democratic practices and principles and act in accordance with the rule of law. In this regard, the responsibility lies squarely on both the government and the governed. Between the lines, this was the message in the sermon of Archbishop Charles Gabriel Palmer-Buckle, the metropolitan archbishop of Accra, to the bar and bench of Ghana on June 29, 2007.

It is good to institutionalize and commemorate occasions and occurrences that leave worthy landmarks. There is a paramount need to candidly identify those things that are evil and undesirable in the Ghanaian national life and throw them away, lest these become institutionalized and a source of constant reminders of bitterness.

The Council of State

Article 89 (1) of the Constitution provides that "there shall be a Council of State to counsel the President in the performance of his functions." But in its composition and operation, the Council of State is virtually a part of the presidency. The Council of State comprises about twenty-five members made up of the following:

a.   Three persons, each one of whom had held the office of (i) chief justice of Ghana, (ii) chief of defense staff, and (iii) inspector general of police. The appointment of these members shall be by the president in consultation with Parliament.

b.   The president of the National House of Chiefs.

c.   One representative from each region of Ghana whose election must be organized and supervised by the Electoral Commission under Article 51 of the Constitution, whereby two representatives from each District Assembly form a regional electoral college.

d.   Eleven other members appointed by the president.

The Council of State advises the government on matters referred to it by the president or Parliament. The Council of State advises the president on important appointments (14). The Constitution requires that the chairman of the council be elected from among themselves, and they carry on deliberations when more than half their number is present. They meet not less than four times in a year normally, but the president or Parliament can convene the Council of State anytime, as the need arises. The council regulates the conduct of its own deliberations, but its decision is by the majority. Any five of the members of the Council of State together can convene the council.

The human specie is a tyrant by nature and would always want, with the least opportunity, to subjugate his fellow man to his personal advantage and/or survival. It is this tyrannical streak in man that enables him, for instance, to derive pleasure in participating in or watching blood sport, such as game hunting, wrestling, and boxing tournaments, which require deliberate violence and drawing the blood of a quarry or opponent. It is in this wise that the Council of State is intended as a buffer institution to check excesses of presidential power. Under the 1992 Constitution, the influence and functions of the Council of State are quite weighty, and when one considers its functions with regard to the amendment of the entrenched clauses under Article 290 of the Constitution together, the caliber of persons who should constitute the Council of State cannot be taken lightly. Therefore, if it happens to be packed with cronies of the president and/or party fanatics and the inordinate faithfuls who are bound to be indulgent for being put there, there is imminent danger of tyrannical dictatorship.

Considering the power of appointment the president exercises in composing the membership of the Council of State, it is submitted that the Council of State as constituted under the 1992 Constitution cannot further the cause of constitutionalism as it is envisioned to do. Regarding the composition of the council under Article 89, even the only four ex officio members of the council are chosen at the discretion of the president where there is more than one eligible ex officio member to be chosen from. For instance, the most recent past inspector general of police who was most clearly not of the ruling party was overlooked for the appointment, while the one chosen was IGP for only a short spell in the short-lived Limann administration.

Upon closer scrutiny, the four governments of the fourth republic have tended to handpick personalities who are quite obviously in favour of the ruling party's political line as members of the Council of State. Furthermore, it is apparent that the election of regional representatives to the council has proved to be a purely partisan political party matter in practice. This does not auger well for developing the Council of State into the kind of institution that can effectively perform its constitutional task of checking the excesses of the presidency and any propensity toward arbitrariness and dictatorship. On top of that, the president has more discretionary power under the Constitution to appoint eleven additional members to the council. This easily tilts the balance of power by numbers in favour of the executive, erasing the effective neutrality of the council and rendering it functionally superfluous.

In view of the grave responsibilities of the council and how best it could carry them out, it is recommended that necessary amendments of Article 89 of the 1992 Constitution be effected to completely remove presidential discretion in appointing members of the Council of State. It is only in this way that the Council of State can function as an effective check for the further advancement of constitutionalism in Ghana and not a seeming "rubber stamp" institution.

The Judiciary

By Articles 125 and 127 of the Constitution, justice emanates from the people and shall be administered by the judiciary in the name of the republic. The judiciary shall be independent in exercising the judicial power vested in it. The chief justice (the head of the judiciary) and other judicial officers exercising judicial power are not subject to any interference whatsoever from any quarters. Although the members of the judiciary are normally appointed by the president, the Parliament, and the Council of State, once appointed, a judicial officer shall not be subject to any interference by those appointing authorities in any matter, whether civil or criminal. The judiciary comprises the Superior Courts of Judicature, namely:

i. the Supreme Court
ii. the Court of Appeals
iii. the High Court and Regional Tribunals and such other courts and tribunals as Parliament may establish

The Superior Courts shall be the Superior Courts of Record, which shall have power to commit contemnors to themselves. And subject to the normal audit of the auditor-general, the financial administration of the judiciary is not subject to any external control or interference.

The foregoing provisions substantially echo the basic principles of the rule of law. The principle of the rule of law means also that law must rule. Only the courts must be left free to interpret the law as they find it, without any interference from anywhere else, than the courts in their hierarchy. It is the rule of law and not the rule of good law: whatever the law, it must rule—whether good or bad. For this reason, the Constitution provides elaborately as to the caliber and the qualification of judges.

To qualify for appointment as a justice of the Supreme Court, the candidate must be a lawyer of proven integrity and high moral character. He must have been a lawyer for fourteen years. For the Court of Appeals appointment, the lawyer qualified must be a lawyer for twelve years. And for the High Court and chairman of the Regional Tribunals, ten years' standing as a lawyer is required. In all cases, the lawyer must be of a high moral character (15) and proven integrity. It will be noted, however, that the citizenry from whom the judges will emerge also have very invaluable part to play or contribution to make toward the realization of the rule of law. The argument here is that the moral strength and integrity must be seen to go around (16). It must include one's disposition and attitude toward all ethnic groups and genders and not limited to only economic and financial disposition. We are adverting to the requisite standard or measure.

It also presupposes the facultative disposition of the Ghanaian citizenry and the factors that go toward determining this disposition in the appointing authority as well as the appointee. Here, one cannot go beyond limited human and mundane factors that are our inevitable limitations. When he has accepted and assumed the responsible office as a judicial officer, a judge has to cope with some necessary restrictions in his personal lifestyle. One example is that he cannot ordinarily walk into a beer parlor to enjoy himself. He then enjoys a tenure of office, remuneration, and retirement benefits lined up for him under Chapter 11 of the Constitution. There is a judicial council comprising eighteen wise men under the chairmanship of the chief justice to study, discuss, and make suggestions for reforms to enhance the chances for his efficient administration of justice.

To facilitate efficient administration of justice, it would appear that Article 128 (1) of the Constitution is elastic. The provision is as follows:

> 128 (1) The Supreme Court shall consist of the Chief Justice and not less than nine justices of the Supreme Court.

This provision gives the president or government the power to rather whimsically appoint a limitless number of Supreme Court justices. It is suggested that the word *more* should replace the word *less* in Article 128 (1). It is absolutely necessary that the Constitution should place the government and any individual citizen or group or party on the same or equal level ground as far as litigating any matter is concerned. Article 128 (1) of the Constitution, as it stands, derogates from that. It is therefore hereby suggested that a new Article 128 (1) should replace the present Article 128 (1) as follows:

> 128 (1) The Supreme Court shall comprise the chief justice and not more than *eight* or *ten* other justices of the Supreme Court. It is necessary to have the total number an odd figure so that where there is a need for the justices of the Supreme Court to decide on any issue by majority, there should be no deadlock. It should not be in all matters that the chief justice should have a prerogative power to decide alone on an issue. The decision to elevate any justice of the superior court of judicature to the Supreme Court, for example, should be a suggestion of the Supreme Court and not the chief justice to the presidency through the Judicial Council.

Chapter Ten

PUBLIC FINANCE

Control of Public Funds

Because governance of today goes beyond the maintenance of law and order and the defense of the sovereignty and territorial integrity of the nation against attacks from both within and outside, modern government has become a complex business. Thus, most of the powers of government are delegated to institutions into which persons are appointed. More than before, modern government is more concerned also with social and economic matters that aim at improving the quality of life to be enjoyed by the people. Therefore, modern government involves a lot of expenditure. This underpins the need first for governments to raise revenue and then to control the outlay of such public funds.

Every person who earns income is liable to pay tax. But there is no taxation except by the authority of an Act of Parliament. In addition, it is only Parliament that can vary or waive any person's tax liability. The revenue generated by the collection of taxes becomes the public funds at the disposal of the government. They comprise all revenues or monies raised or received from and on behalf of the government as well as monies raised or received in trust for or on behalf of the government. These constitute the consolidated fund. There is also a contingency fund. Besides these, there are also other funds, and the Bank of Ghana (the central bank) is, by law, the sole custodian of state funds (1).

The Central Bank—Bank of Ghana

The sole custodian of state funds is the Bank of Ghana. It is the central bank and is solely owned by the government of Ghana. The bank can only authorize any other person or authority to act as custodian of any specific public fund by notice published in the gazette.

The Bank of Ghana is the authority that regulates and controls the banking system and credit policy to promote healthy economic development and efficient utilization of the resources of Ghana. It is therefore the bankers' bank. In all cases, there can be no withdrawal from the consolidated fund, except to meet expenditure that is charged on the fund and by estimates approved by resolution of Parliament. So that in the case of the judiciary, the chief justice, in consultation with the Judicial Council, causes the estimates of expenditure and estimates of development expenditure of the judiciary to be submitted to the president not later than two months before the end of each financial year. The president will then cause the estimates to be laid before Parliament, and if it is approved by Parliament, the estimates will then be charged on the consolidated fund (2). While the public debt of Ghana shall be charged on the consolidated fund and other public funds, only a resolution of Parliament can authorize the government to enter into agreement for the granting of a loan out of any public fund or account (3). Thus, the Bank of Ghana shall be the only authority to issue the currency of Ghana. No other authority has power to issue the currency except the Bank of Ghana.

The Governor of the Bank of Ghana

The governor of the Bank of Ghana is the controller of transactions involving directly or indirectly any transfer involving foreign exchange whether within or outside the country. When the said transfer of foreign exchange is contrary to law, the governor shall disallow it.

The president, in consultation with the Council of State, shall appoint the governor of the Bank of Ghana for a term of four years. He is exempted from the operation of Article 285 of the Constitution, which bars any person from being appointed as the chairman of any public corporation who holds a position therein and therefore the chairman of the governing body of the Bank of Ghana (the central bank). His conditions of service are the same as those of a justice of the Supreme Court (4), and his emolument shall not be reduced while he continues to hold the office of governor, except that the Parliamentary Committee responsible for financial measures shall monitor the foreign receipt and payments or transfers of the Bank of Ghana in and outside Ghana and shall report on them to Parliament once every six months. The Bank of Ghana itself is enjoined to submit to the auditor-general for audit, a statement of its foreign exchange receipts, and payments for transfers in and outside Ghana after the end of the first six months of the financial year, which the auditor-general shall submit his report thereon to Parliament for necessary action.

Government Statistician

The statistical service provides data for planning and formulation of policies. The head of the Statistical Service is the government statistician, appointed by the president in consultation with the Council of State. And there is also a Statistical Service Board of not more than five members and a chairman (i.e., six members including the chairman). All the six members are appointees of the president by merit of their expert knowledge. Again, the president will consult the Council of State and the government statistician on these appointments. Together they are responsible for the collection, compilation, analyses, and publication of socioeconomic data on Ghana necessary for planning etc.

Auditor-General

The name of the auditor-general appears in every book in every institution whose functions involve an expenditure of money at all. It is important to protect public funds. Thus, the accounts of Ghana and all public offices—including the courts, the various government administrations, universities, and in fact, all public institutions—are subject to auditing by the auditor-general under the Constitution.

By Article 187 of the 1992 Constitution, the auditor-general or any person authorized or appointed by him shall have access to all books, records, returns, and other documents relevant or relating to the accounts of all public institutions and organs for the purpose of auditing same and reporting thereon. And it is the auditor-general who has the authority to approve the form in which the accounts of all public institutions and organizations shall be kept. The auditor-general shall by law submit his audit report on any public account to Parliament six months after the end of the financial year preceding. The report shall draw attention to anything that, in his opinion, constitutes irregularity. Parliament shall then debate the report of the auditor-general. In carrying out his functions, the auditor-general shall not be subject to the direction and control of any other person or authority. He will be absolutely independent. Any aggrieved person may appeal to the High Court on any aspect of the auditor-general's report. The accounts and expenses of the auditor-general, in performance of his functions, are charged on the consolidated fund. By Article 187 (15) of the Constitution, the account of the auditor-general shall be audited and reported on by an auditor appointed by Parliament. The auditor-general, the head of the Civil Service or his representative, and five members, including its chairman, comprise the Audit Service Board. The president, in consultation with the Council of State, appoints the chairman and the four other members of the Audit Service Board. The Audit Service Board in turn appoints other officers of the Audit Service in consultation with the Public Services Commission.

Chapter Eleven

PUBLIC SERVICES

(Chapter 14 of the Constitution)

Freedom and Independence of the Media

Democratic freedom or multiparty democracy cannot exist in the absence of press freedom or independence of the media. In this vein, the 1992 Constitution guarantees the freedom and independence of the media (1). There is also the need that the media must be vigorous. There is express provision that there shall be no censorship in Ghana among many other express guarantees for free press and independent media. However, these guarantees are subject to laws that are "reasonably required in the interest of national security, public order, public morality and for the purposes of protecting the reputation, rights and freedoms of other persons." At the same time, Article 165 provides that the provisions in Article 164 shall not be taken to limit the enjoyment of any of the fundamental human rights and freedoms guaranteed under Chapter 5 of the Constitution. One would think that there is the law of libel and there is liability for injurious falsehood.

It is not always easy to formulate or define morality. *Public security* and *public order* are authoritative terms. It would have sounded safer if the Constitution had reminded us that media practitioners should be aware of the laws protecting other people's rights and reputations. The law of sedition is still one of the statutes of Ghana, only that liberal democracy does not favour its gleeful use. This is where it should be recognized that the quality of the citizenry, as well as the benevolence that will be displayed in toleration by those in authority, would animate those provisions. Rights always go with responsibilities. However, the establishment of the National Media Commission of eighteen members, to include representatives of (among other groups) media practitioners themselves, is heartwarming. The Media Commission also includes writers, religious bodies, bar association, women's groups, etc. The commission is to promote freedom and independence of the media and ensure mass communication or dissemination of information without inhibitions of any kind.

The National Media Commission is also charged with making regulations by constitutional instrument for registration of newspapers and other publications. There are provisions safeguarding the tenure of office of media practitioners in the state media organizations without exercising any control over the professional function of practitioners (2).

National Commission for Civic Education

After the 1966 coup d'état, there was a feeling, rightly or wrongly, that the people of Ghana did not know their civic rights and responsibilities. It was found necessary, therefore, to set up a centre for civic education to teach Ghanaians their civic rights. The truth is that people often neglect or refuse to assume their responsibilities, but they always want to enjoy their rights. The National Commission on Civic Education (NCCE) is conceived to create and sustain within the society the awareness of the principles and objectives of the Constitution and make the people conscious that the Constitution is the fundamental law of the land.

The NCCE is assigned the function of educating and encouraging the public to defend the Constitution against abuses. It is also to be able to prevent abuses. In this assignment, the commission has responsibility to formulate, from time to time, programmes at all levels of national life for the consideration of government toward realizing the objectives of the Constitution and possibly preventing their abuse.

The commission is a public service institution, and therefore, its staff is subject to the usual tenets of public service appointments (3). In essence, however, the activities of the National Commission for Civic Education may be taken to be supplementary to the normal education of the citizenry with special emphasis on adult education. It should not be an organization for the purpose of seeking to entrench or supplant any particular culture as an ideal in Ghana, for that cannot be civic education. It is cultural imposition (4).

Commission on Human Rights and Administrative Justice (Articles 216–230)

This institution is quasi-judicial. It is headed by a commissioner for human rights and administrative justice and assisted by two deputies. The commissioner has the status of a Court of Appeals judge, and the two deputies are constitutionally accorded with the status of justices of the High Court. This commission is to have regional and district branches throughout the country. Its functions include receiving and investigating complaints. The commission will investigate complaints of violations concerning the functioning of the Public Services Commission and complaints about practices and actions by persons in private enterprise. It has power to negotiate settlement as well as power to bring proceedings in court to remedy the complaints investigated by it.

The Commission on Human Rights and Administrative Justice (CHRAJ) can also report its findings to the attorney general. Thus, this commission can be likened to the Ombudsman in its functions. However, it cannot investigate any matter that is pending before any court nor any matter involving the government of Ghana and another government. Subject to any act of Parliament, the commission has power to make, by constitutional instrument, regulations regarding the manner and procedure for bringing complaints before it and how to investigate complaints before it. The president appoints the members of the commission under Article 70 of the Constitution, i.e., acting on the advice of the Council of State.

The Public Services

(Chapter 14 of the Constitution)

All public institutions, to which government appoints personnel and whose activities and finances are responsive to the consolidated fund or any other public fund, constitute the Public Services of Ghana. As such, all appointments under Article 190 of the Constitution are public service appointments. They include the Civil Service, Judicial Service, Audit Service, Education Service, and all institutions under Article 190 and other public corporations not meant to be commercial ventures, as well as other public institutions established by Acts of Parliament under Article 192, with provisions in the acts creating them pertaining to themselves. And Article 193 empowers the president to appoint a public officer as the head of the Civil Service. The chairman, vice chairman, and three other members of the Public Services Commission are full-time members of the commission. There may be such other members as Parliament may prescribe. They must be persons qualified to be elected as members of Parliament and not otherwise disqualified from holding public office. Their salaries and allowances and remunerations are to be determined by the president upon the recommendation of a committee of not more than five persons appointed by the president acting on the advice of the Council of State, as under Article 71 of the Constitution. The Public Services Commission shall not be subject to the control or direction of any person or authority in the performance of its functions (5). The president, in whom the power of appointment is vested, also reserves the power to delegate in writing his power of appointment to the governing council concerned or to a committee or to any member of that committee of the governing council.

By Article 11 of the Constitution, statutes such as the Police Service Act, the Prisons Service Act, and the Armed Forces Act have been legitimized and brought into the ambit of the Constitution. Therefore, their various heads—namely, the inspector general of police (IGP) respecting the Police Service, the director general of the Prisons Service, and the chief of defense staff of the Ghana Armed Forces respectively—and their various governing councils are covered by Articles 200–204 (Chapter 15) and Articles 205–209 (Chapter 17) of the Constitution. The laws governing Immigration Service and the Customs Excise and Prevention Service must be taken as having been legitimized by this Constitution.

In all this, it should be noted that the president is the one who wields, in his consultation with the Council of State, enormous powers of appointment, subject though, in some cases, to Parliamentary approval. On the whole, the presidency is rather too powerful. The Constitution needs to be wholly amended.

CHAPTER TWELVE

LOCAL GOVERNMENT

(Chapter 20 of the Constitution)

The Local Government System

The local government system under the Constitution of 1992 is one of the landmarks of these constitutional provisions, for it is a desirably decentralized system aiming at enabling every citizen, even of the remotest part of Ghana, to feel the impact of government as much as is possible. It has to be accepted that this is one of the progressive and ideal gains from the long leadership spell of Flight Lieutenant Rawlings, any shortcomings notwithstanding, that Ghanaians can be proud of.

The whole country is divided into administrative districts, and each district has its own District Assembly, while the big towns and cities have Metropolitan Assemblies. A district or metropolitan assembly is the highest local political authority with deliberative, legislative, and executive powers. Each district is divided into a number of local government electoral areas within the district. The District Assembly comprises the following:

    a.   One person from each local government electoral area within that district within the District Assembly's area of authority, though without a vote in the assembly

b.   The district chief executive (DCE)
c.   Other members appointed by the president in consultation with the traditional authorities and other interest groups in the district

Apparently, the identification of the interest groups is a matter for the president (1). The election of a District Assembly member is by universal adult suffrage without political parties. The district chief executive is an appointee of the president with the prior approval of the members of the District Assembly by two-thirds majority of members present and voting. The DCE presides over the executive committee of the District Assembly and is responsible for the day-to-day executive and administrative functions of the assembly. The DCE is also the chief representative of the central government in the district. There is a presiding member of the District Assembly elected from among them. He presides over the assembly's meetings (2).

Functions

The District Assemblies levy and collect taxes, rates, duties, and other fees and formulate and devise modes of executing plans and strategies for effective mobilization of the resources necessary for the overall development of the districts. Other functions of the District Assemblies may be prescribed by Parliament.

Revenue

The District Assembly derives its revenue from the central government, which is constitutionally required to make available 5 percent of the revenue accruing to Ghana to the District Assemblies. This is paid into a District Assembly's common fund in quarterly installments. However, the District Assembly may also benefit from any grant in aid from any quarters. The funds of the District Assembly are subject to the auditor-general's annual examination. There is a District Assembly common fund administrator, who is an appointee of the central government, i.e., the president (3). The regional minister for each region is the chairman of the Regional Coordinating Council, comprising the following:

a. The regional minister and his deputy(ies)
b. The presiding member and district chief executive of each district in the region
c. Two chiefs from the Regional House of Chiefs
d. Regional heads of the ministries decentralized in the region as members without voting rights (decentralized in the sense that subject to the Constitution, the regional heads of ministries do not need clearance from the central government in Accra for every administrative decision)

CHAPTER THIRTEEN

LANDS AND MINERAL RESOURCES OF GHANA

(Chapter 21 of the Constitution)

The 1992 Constitution is particular about the country's land and mineral resources. In Ghana, there are individually owned lands. Some of these lands have become family lands on the death of the individual owners. There are public lands vested in the state/president that is held in trust for and on behalf of the people, and there are stool lands that belong to chieftaincy stools or skins for the benefit of those who are subjects of those stools or skins. These are generally referred to as stool lands. Stool lands are not found in every part of Ghana, and there are no public lands in the Northern, Upper East, and Upper West Regions (1). Every mineral in its natural state in, under, or upon any land in Ghana; rivers, streams, water courses throughout Ghana; the exclusive economic zone; and any area covered by the territorial sea or continental shelf is the property of the Republic of Ghana and is vested in the president and held in trust for the people of Ghana. There is a Lands Commission that, in coordination with the relevant public agencies and government bodies, (a) manage public lands vested in the state, (b) advise the government and local authorities on government policies in particular areas, (c) formulate and submit recommendations with respect to land use and capability,

(d) advise and assist in registration of title to land, and (e) perform other functions assigned to it by the minister responsible for lands and natural resources. There is a branch of the Lands Commission in every region, with the regional lands officer as its secretary.

Land Ownership and Noncitizens

A noncitizen of Ghana cannot have a freehold interest or fee simple of land in Ghana. An agreement, deed, or conveyance of any kind that seeks to confer on a person who is not a citizen of Ghana any title in fee simple or freehold interest over any land is void (2). If a non-Ghanaian happened to have a freehold interest in any land in Ghana on August 22, 1969, that interest or right shall be deemed to be a leasehold interest for a period of fifty years at a peppercorn rent commencing from August 22, 1969, and the freehold reversionary interest shall vest in the president on behalf of and in trust for the people of Ghana. No interest in or right over any land in Ghana shall be created that vests in a person who is not a citizen of Ghana a leasehold for a term longer than fifty years at any one time. If it was done by August 22, 1969, it will be deemed to be for a period of fifty years commencing from August 22, 1969.

Stool and Skin Land Properties

All stool lands are vested in the appropriate stool or skin for the subjects of the stool or skin. There is an administrator of stool lands whose responsibility includes the establishment and keeping of stool lands accounts for each stool, into which is paid all rent dues, royalties, revenues, or other payments accruing from the stool land. The administrator of stool lands is responsible for collecting and paying those monies into stool lands accounts and also disbursing same in accordance with a prescribed formula as follows:

a.   Ten percent to the office of the administrator of stool lands to cover administrative expenses
b.   Twenty-five percent of the remaining goes to the stool through the traditional authority

c. Fifty-five percent goes to the District Assembly of the area

This formula shows that the 10 percent of the stool lands revenue that goes to the administrator is charged on the total revenue first. The remaining, which is 90 percent of the total, is now distributed according to the above formula (2). The Constitution, by its Article 268 and 169, provides for the protection of the nation's natural resources.

CHIEFTAINCY

(Chapter 22 of the Constitution)

The 1992 Constitution has declared that "the institution of Chieftaincy together with its Traditional Councils as established by Customary Law and usage is hereby guaranteed."

By Article 277, however, *chief* has been defined as "a person, who, hailing from the appropriate family and lineage, has been validly nominated, elected, or selected and enstooled/enskinned or installed as a chief or queen mother in accordance with the relevant Customary Law and usage." It is submitted that the definition above will pose problems of construction for the courts when they have to adjudicate in a dispute as to the validity of the process. This is because the process of selection or election is not the same. While a nomination can amount to a selection, an election cannot. Besides, it is only when the traditional processes have all been faithfully met that there can be validity. In Ghanaian traditional systems of chieftaincy where several families and lineages claim the office of chieftaincy, who does the nomination or selection? Thus, a selection will apply only where there is no rival claim, or else, there would be arbitrariness. However, Articles 26 (2) and 39 (2) of the Constitution would seem to be against arbitrariness. So the three words—i.e., *validly*, *selected*, and *nominated*—need not be there, especially when the Constitution does not say that "or selected . . .

where there is no other contestant . . ." In effect, it is suggested that in Ghana, as constitutionally recognized, the designation "chief" must mean a person, who, hailing from the appropriate family and lineage, has been in accordance with the relevant customary law and usage, nominated, elected, and enstooled or enskinned and traditionally installed as a leader of a group of persons of an area who are subjects of that traditional stool or skin as their symbol of leadership. This definition must also apply to the designation "queen mother." Chief in Nigeria is a republican title acquired or sometimes attained by the individual in a locality or community.

Thus, by Chapter 22 of the Constitution, chieftaincy matters involving processes leading to the installation of a chief are left for the attention of the National House of Chiefs, as constituted under Article 271 to perform functions set out under Articles 272 and 273 and Regional Houses of Chiefs under Article 274. While a chief can hold any public office in Ghana, no chief can be a member of Parliament or partake in partisan politics. This is quite in good place since, in Ghana, Parliament is a House of Commons. Chiefs have their place in Ghana, but not in Parliament and not in party politics.

Conclusion

Ghana's constitutional journey had started in the Gold Coast in 1844, arriving in the Republic of Ghana in 1992. But events in Nigeria seem to indicate that that country has still not arrived. Until they substitute the word *domicile* for the word *indigene* in their national and constitutional vocabulary, there still would continue to be problems and obstacles.

The constitutional provisions of the Republic of Ghana (1992) are comprehensive, covering as they are the need to regulate the exercise of power to the extent that Articles 278–283 of the Constitution have provided for the regulation of governmental power. A Commission of Inquiry is set up only when the president is satisfied that there is a need or when the Council of State so advises or when a parliamentary resolution to the president specifies matters to be probed. Then in appointing personnel to handle the probing, the president's powers in that direction are not at large or whimsical.

Then there is a code of conduct for public officers stating in broad outlines including compulsory declaration of assets before and after assumption of office (1).

There are provisions—the entrenched clauses specified in Article 290— which cannot be amended without referendum, and there are clauses not entrenched that require less stringent procedures for amendment (2). The Constitution has effectively placed the government on the same plane or scale with any individual, making a claim against the state by abolishing in effect the erstwhile State Proceedings Act, which, hitherto, compelled a claimant against the state to obtain a fiat before suing a parastatal or government (3). Crowning it all is a set of smooth transitional provisions.

Nigeria, too, would probably have shot up politically and constitutionally in 1993 had there not been an abortion of the system by Ibrahim Babangida in June of that year. In 1993, the decision to hold general and presidential elections in Nigeria was a political decision by Babangida as a military dictator, so to stop it at any stage by the same person was equally political. Therefore, it was clearly improper to involve the judiciary in that feat. It was cowardice as it was dishonest to go to court to ask for any order to stop it or cancel the presidential election when the electoral law made by himself clearly ousted the jurisdiction of the courts in the matter.

Arbitrary Disqualification of Candidates—Nigeria

The same Babangida as the military ruler had whimsically and arbitrarily disqualified and denied to some persons their right to seek the mandate of the people to be president. He did not go to court to do that. Nor did he give any reasons for doing so. Thus, the strange court order of June 10, 1993, attracted so much outrage. Reaction to it was so hysterical that other

High Courts in other states throughout the Nigerian federation resorted to similar orders and counterorders in protest, which almost brought the High Courts in the different states into ridicule in the confusion that Babangida created.

Patriotic Vision

Patriotic vision is the light in which one sees one's environment or one's country. Ghanaians have been lucky not to have lost their collective patriotic vision. Ghanaians have also been lucky to have an enlightened public opinion that can be united when the need arises and was indeed united on issues, unlike Nigeria, where the innate ethnicity has been rather so endemic that the patriotic vision of the citizenry has been blunted and corrupted and rendered perverse and inarticulate among the professional classes, especially the Nigerian lawyers who pervert and belabor perverse logic to justify mischief. So that political power is always with a cabal in Nigeria, people pervert logic to make sure that things never change.

President Obasanjo's failed attempt to change the 1999 Constitution in order to remain in office for a third term was one of the results of misleading bootlicking of blatant sycophantic cronies. The tendency has been to suggest dictatorial situations by one news media or another to the incumbent leader, which only a person of a strong moral character can reject. It is in this vein that claims in the press that President Kufuor desired to change the constitutional arrangement of an elected vice president alongside the president to a prime minister appointed by the president was happily denied by President Kufuor. Ghanaians are not mere pupils to whom a bad teacher can suggest sickness by entering the classroom and announcing that he has a headache. This kind of situation must not be encouraged to happen again.

Suggestions

The Constitution of the Republic of Ghana (1992) is a landmark document. The successive future governments of the country and the Ghanaian people are the ones on whom the responsibility lies for its preservation. In other words, the effectiveness of Articles 2 and 3 inculcating and urging fearlessness in the citizenry is a function of the future conduct of the government and the governed. This is because if the Constitution is ever effectively overthrown, there cannot be any resistance to its overthrow. Therefore, Articles 2 and 3 provisions are not enough since the virtues of courage and fearlessness can go around. These virtues can be available to the loyal citizen as well as the reckless adventurist of a soldier. The effective desirable conduct is the avoidance of all inimical acts of both the government and the governed. A line in our national anthem prays to God to help us resist oppressor's rule. Perhaps we should add, too, that God might help us to prevent oppressor's rule. For when a people or sections of them perceive that they are being oppressed, Article 3 of the Constitution would be of no avail. The courageous, loyal, good citizen as well as the reckless adventurists will claim to be acting with the animation of patriotism. So constant approbatory conduct from both the government and the governed is the craving.

To facilitate this, it is hereby suggested that Article 89, the provision for the composition and function of the Council of State, be amended because in its present composition, the Council of State appears to be unwieldy, and also, the provision gives to Mr. President too much discretionary power of appointment into that council. The presidency cannot be taken to be devoid of the normal human streak. There is a need to increase the number of ex officio members of the Council of State under Article 89 (2) (a) and reduce the number of presidential appointees under Article 89 (2) (d) or probably abolish (d) altogether in order to secure a thorough constitutionalism.

There is also a need to provide expressly that the regional representatives on the Council of State shall be elected absolutely without any involvement of the political parties. They should be elected solely on the strength of their individual personal standing and qualities. With the presidency and Parliament being partisan institutions, only a nonpartisan Council of State will provide the needed checks and balances for effective constitutionalism. It may also be necessary to provide for the president to be obliged with the advice of the Council of State on any issue. In a similar vein, it is hereby seriously suggested that Article 78 (1) be amended by deleting the provision that the majority of Cabinet ministers be chosen from members of Parliament and substituting therefor a provision that Cabinet ministers of state shall be chosen from members of the public with the prior approval of Parliament. Therefore, a member of Parliament who has accepted ministerial appointment shall forthwith resign from his position of membership of Parliament. This will facilitate a full realization of the principle of separation of powers for achieving full constitutionalism in Ghana. It is necessary to obviate any inducement, desire, or tendency of members of Parliament to actually or apparently seek to work themselves into the good books of Mr. President for possible ministerial appointments, thereby compromising the articulation on issues as members of Parliament.

In sum, the suggested amendments include the following:

1. *Citizenship*
   The effects of Articles 6–9 (3): 62 (a) on citizenship should be reexamined.

2. *The esprit de corps*
   The election of the president, i.e., Article 63 (3), should be such that it must satisfy a compelling need to develop, promote, nurture, and sustain the esprit de corps. It is suggested that in general elections, it should be provided that the successful candidate to be president must win not less than, at least, two presidential constituencies in each region of Ghana, and only where more than one candidate satisfies this condition or requirement or where no candidate satisfies the requirement of winning at least two presidential constituencies in each region, then the successful candidate to be president must secure more than 50 percent of the total votes cast in the presidential election. It should be necessary to prevent a situation where there could be virtual or actual regional or ethnic domination.

3. *Separation of powers*

   Articles 78 relating to the appointment of Cabinet ministers and 89 on the membership of the Council of State need amendments. The Ghanaian presidency is too powerful. The Constitution should therefore be amended on the whole to avoid subjective provisions and articles like that on the Electoral Commission.

4. *The judiciary*

   Article 128 (1) relating to the number of Supreme Court justices should not be more than nine, including the chief justice, so that the president or government cannot appoint any new Supreme Court justice or elevate any judge to the Supreme Court unless there is a vacancy.

INDEX